People

STYLES
OF THE
STARS

STAFF FOR THIS BOOK

EDITOR: Eric Levin

SENIOR EDITOR: Richard Burgheim

ART DIRECTOR: Tony Limuaco

PICTURE EDITOR: Gail Toivanen

CHIEF OF REPORTERS: Denise Lynch

WRITER: Allison Adato

DESIGNER: Rob Yagley

COPY EDITOR: Lance Kaplan

OPERATIONS: Gavin Smith

Special thanks to: Alan Anuskiewicz, Jane Bealer, Will Becker, Robert Britton, Betsy Castillo, Sal Covarrubias, Orpha Davis, Nancy Eils, Helene Elek, Brien Foy, Marjorie Frohlinger, George Hill, Joshua Himwich, Suzy Im, Bonnie Johnson, Jonathan Michals, Eric Mischel, James Oberman, Stan Olson, Stephen Pabarue, Hilli Pitzer, Susan Radlauer, Gabrielle Reiffel, Helen Russell, Cynthia Sanz, John Silva, Jill Smolowe, Elizabeth Sporkin, Jonathan Vasata, Constance White, Céline Wojtala

Copyright ©2001 Time Inc. Home Entertainment
Published by

Time Inc.
1271 Avenue of the Americas
New York, NY 10020

PRESIDENT: Rob Gursha
VICE PRESIDENT, BRANDED BUSINESSES: David Arfine
EXECUTIVE DIRECTOR, MARKETING SERVICES: Carol Pittard
DIRECTOR, RETAIL & SPECIAL SALES: Tom Mifsud
DIRECTOR OF FINANCE: Tricia Griffin
MARKETING DIRECTOR: Kenneth Maehlum
MARKETING DIRECTOR: Maarten Terry
PRODUCT MANAGER: Dennis Sheehan
EDITORIAL OPERATIONS MANAGER: John Calvano
ASSOCIATE PRODUCT MANAGER: Sara Stumpf
ASSISTANT PRODUCT MANAGER: Linda Frisbie

Special thanks to: Victoria Alfonso, Suzanne DeBenedetto, Robert Dente, Gina Di Meglio, Peter Harper, Roberta Harris, Natalie McCrea, Jessica McGrath, Jonathan Polsky, Emily Rabin, Mary Jane Rigoroso, Steven Sandonato, Tara Sheehan, Meredith Shelley, Bozena Szwagulinski, Marina Weinstein, Niki Whelan

First Edition

ISBN: 1-929049-69-2
Library of Congress Control Number: 2001091488

People Books is a trademark of Time Inc.

We welcome your comments and suggestions about People Books.
Please write to us at:
People Books
Attention: Book Editors
P.O. Box 11016
Des Moines, IA 50336-1016

If you would like to order any of our hardcover Collector's Edition books, please call us at 1-800-327-6388
(Monday through Friday, 7:00 a.m.–8:00 p.m. or Saturday, 7:00 a.m.–6:00 p.m. Central Time).
Please visit our Web site at www.TimeBookstore.com

PRINTED IN THE UNITED STATES OF AMERICA

PRECEDING PAGE: Teen queen Christina Aguilera turned the century—and heads—in 2000.

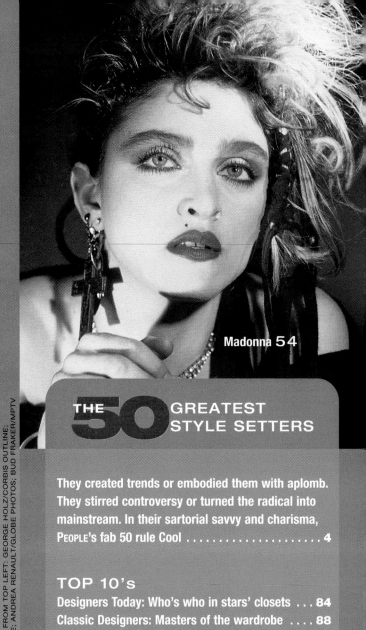

Madonna 54

PRECEDING PAGE: BERNARD KUHMSTEDT/CORBIS OUTLINE. THIS SPREAD, CLOCKWISE FROM TOP LEFT: GEORGE HOLZ/CORBIS OUTLINE; FRANK OCKENFELS/MPTV; GEORGE HURRELL/MPTV; MICHAEL BORUM/CORBIS OUTLINE; ANDREA RENAULT/GLOBE PHOTOS; BUD FRAKER/MPTV

THE 50 GREATEST STYLE SETTERS

They created trends or embodied them with aplomb. They stirred controversy or turned the radical into mainstream. In their sartorial savvy and charisma, PEOPLE's fab 50 rule Cool 4

TOP 10's

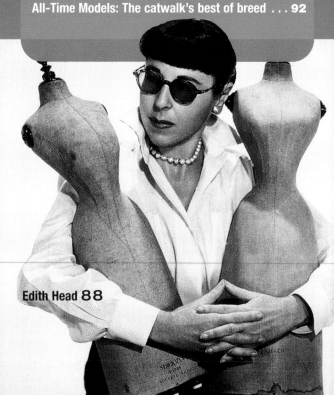

Edith Head 88

Sarah Michelle Gellar 96

Jean Harlow 105

CONTENTS

Sean Combs 122

Dolly Parton & Co. 135

People weekly 50

GREATEST STYLE SETTERS

The best-dressed? Not always. (Some made the list for barely wearing a stitch.) But these are the celebs whose trailblazing taste defined their time and changed the look of our lives

When Jackie Kennedy reached for a pillbox hat, it was Hepburn's look (here, in 1966's *How to Steal a Million*) that she was after.

AUDREY HEPBURN

Playful yet sophisticated, she turned heads away from the hourglass figure

"My look is attainable," she asserted in a 1989 interview. "Women can look like Audrey Hepburn by flipping out their hair, buying the large glasses and the little sleeveless dresses." Indeed, when we speak of little black sheaths, or dainty

"In spite of her fragile appearance, she's like steel"
—*Cary Grant*

"She was so exactly *it*," said *Two for the Road* costumer Mary Quant of Hepburn (in 1956). "And 'it' was everything: those exquisite eyes, the witty mouth."

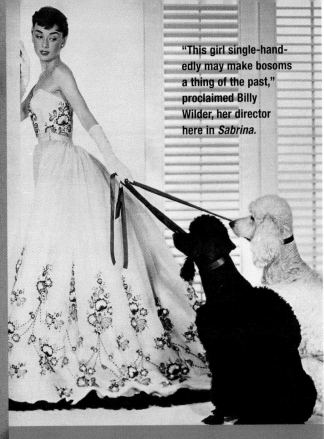

"This girl single-handedly may make bosoms a thing of the past," proclaimed Billy Wilder, her director here in *Sabrina*.

High heels towered over fashion until Hepburn (in 1954) made comfortable ballet flats a stylish option.

"Givenchy outfits gave me 'protection' because I felt so good in them," she said of her designer of 40 years (including *Breakfast at Tiffany's*).

With grace that transcended mere attire, Hepburn spent many of her post-Hollywood years as a UNICEF special ambassador. In 1992 she visited young famine victims in Somalia.

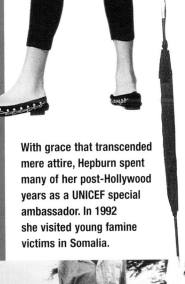

Sabrina heels, what we mean is Audrey Hepburn. But would that it were a mere matter of shopping to duplicate her gamine charm. She had a dancer's frame (5'7" and 110 pounds for most of her life), moved like a ballerina and wore clothes like a model. "She deliberately looked different from other women [and] dramatized her slenderness into her chief asset," said Edith Head. When the costumer met Hepburn, Monroesque curves were the norm, and she tried to give the young actress built-in cleavage. Hepburn refused, choosing what she thought was right for her. Then, once she had enough clout in Hollywood, she asked for Hubert de Givenchy to dress her in 1954's *Sabrina*. Their collaboration was so successful that he outfitted her offscreen as well, in capri pants, ballet flats and collars to show off her elegant neck. Mastering the Hepburn style, she appeared in *They All Laughed* in 1981 in clothes pulled entirely from her own closet. As Givenchy once said of his friend, "Is there a woman who would not want to look like Audrey?"

JACQUELINE KENNEDY ONASSIS

The First Lady of the New Frontier taught a nation about style by graceful example

"I wanted her to stand out like a flower in a field"
—Oleg Cassini

The affianced couple posed in
Hyannis Port in 1953. "The
world has no right," she said,
"to Jack's private life with me."

Jackie (in 1969 with the kids,
sister Lee Radziwill and niece
Anna) was "happiest with her
children," said a pal.

A s a student at Vassar, Jacqueline
Bouvier wrote that her goal was
to be "a sort of Overall Art Director of
the Twentieth Century." Fifteen years
later, just after she left the White House
as a young widow, *Women's Wear
Daily* reflected that Mrs. Kennedy
"probably did more to uplift taste levels
in the United States than any woman in the history of our country." She dressed American, to
please the garment union and boost her husband's image. She dressed for the camera: in bright solids, with large buttons
that read well in pictures. Mostly, she
dressed to be modern. Each streamlined
gown, boxy jacket and pillbox hat
announced a break with the Eisenhower
era, indeed with the first half of the
century. Financing this well-contrived
wardrobe was her father-in-law, Joe
Kennedy. He introduced her to his
friend, designer Oleg Cassini, who
became her official couturier. In the
post-Camelot era, Jackie, by then
Mrs. Onassis, dressed more simply,
retreating into muted colors, and
the hopeful anonymity of a pair of
oversize black sunglasses.

She wore a Cassini wool dress in 1961 (left).

**"She knew exactly what she
needed and how to wear it,"
said Carolina Herrera, who
made the suit at right (1989).**

**"I love the work I do,"
Onassis said of being a
book editor in New York
City. She looked
sweater-set smart at
her desk in 1977.**

PRINCESS DIANA

"The insignificant ugly duckling was obviously going to be a swan"
—*Earl Spencer, Diana's brother*

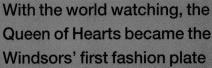

With the world watching, the Queen of Hearts became the Windsors' first fashion plate

Her earliest efforts would not have distinguished her from a long and frumpy line of Windsors. The newly minted Princess of Wales favored busy stripes or polka dots and faux military gear. ("She looks like a lost member of Sgt. Pepper's band," sniped a tabloid.) But with guidance and latent flair, she became a fan of fashion and champion of previously unknown British designers. Whether in suits or one-armed formal gowns, "she broke the barriers of the accepted form of royal dressing," said designer David Sassoon. Not by coincidence, her style changed dramatically with her 1996 divorce. Finally she was free to wear the short lengths that flattered her long legs. One outfit, worn in public the night Charles admitted to adultery in a TV interview, was subsequently called the revenge dress. By then she recognized the power of clothes, and in 1996 exercised it to munificent effect when she auctioned 79 gowns to raise $3.5 million for charity.

At her auction, a guest asked how her gowns had stayed so clean. "I've spilled gravy and shrimps down my front like everybody," she said (left, in '97). "The palace has wonderful cleaners."

By the time she sported this football jacket in '94, Diana had adopted a new wardrobe philosophy: "If it shocks them at the palace, all to the good. It's what they need."

"Early on," said Amanda Wakeley, who outfitted the Princess (at Highgrove in '86), "she was using the clothes to hide her shyness."

Di-watcher Diana Vreeland observed, "She's got radiance. What she wears is incidental" (left, with Wills and Harry in 1988).

Before her 1981 wedding, Diana (in the '94 "revenge" gown) owned only one dress. By the late '80s she had 12 dozen in her closet.

Roberts (in vintage Valentino, accepting her '01 Oscar), kept the micro-minis she wore in *Erin Brockovich*, but didn't immediately venture out in them.

JULIA ROBERTS

She enhances any ensemble with the perfect accessory: Her brilliant smile

"I'm a late-blooming clothes fanatic. Most girls go through this at 16 or 18"

No matter how many more Oscars she wins, or how many "serious" films she makes, the requisite clip for the highlights montage shown at any future Julia Roberts retrospective will be the shopping scene in 1990's *Pretty Woman*. As Roy Orbison, speaking for the audience, wails "Mercy!" over the soundtrack, just watch how she relishes each new outfit, swirling and catching a glimpse of her fabulous self from every angle. Face it, no one's that good an actress. She had to be having a little fun. And she does in real life, too, equally comfy dressing up in favorites like Richard Tyler, Vivienne Tam and Calvin Klein (she's been spotted in the front row of his shows) or roaming her New Mexico ranch in flannel and denim. "I'm in a phase where style is becoming a fun issue, a sporting event," she said in 1997. But even at her 1993 wedding to Lyle Lovett, she exuded the confidence to walk down the aisle in a white gown and bare feet. Not that she doesn't occasionally doubt her appearance. "What?" she once asked rhetorically. "I'm in a movie called *Pretty Woman,* so now I can never think I'm unattractive?" At a down moment, she moaned, "I don't want to change my life, just my butt." Yet her secrets for looking good are maddeningly simple: "As you get older, if you are as blessed as I am and really living the life you want, then happiness sort of becomes your face." A face that, with its famous coast-to-coast smile, brings happiness to moviegoers by the millions.

The actress knit sweaters for ex-beau Benjamin Bratt (together in '98). She likes the sociability of knitting: "I can chat with people and just knit away."

Why is this woman smiling? Roberts (in '97) is Hollywood's first $20 million gal. Her *Brockovich* take: $400,000 a day on-set.

Roberts (in 2001) recalled wearing Garanimals as a kid. "You know, hippos with hippos, giraffes with giraffes . . ."

Only at 30 did Roberts "realize you can be comfortable, stylish and, dare I say, pull a whole sexy thing." She did (right) at a '99 *Notting Hill* premiere.

Knowing what looked good on herself allowed a designer to define "à la mode" for generations to come

By day, young Gabrielle Chanel, who had been orphaned at age 12, sewed in her aunt's dress shop. By night she sang in clubs—her signature song was about a dog named Coco. That was in the early 1900s, when women still wore corsets and long dresses, holdovers from the last century. The clothes might have suited those who had the *belles figures* to squeeze into those silhouettes, but not Chanel. So with help from a man she met at the club, she ventured into design, beginning with simple hats. "I am first and, finally, my only model," she would say, breaking with the tradition of accenting curves and restricting movement. She offered instead jerseys and shorter skirts that flattered her own slim build. They were an instant hit. By World War I she was renowned. She had given women freedom—and the little black dress. The Second World War forced Chanel to close her Paris atelier, but she resumed business in 1953 with another breakthrough: the women's suit, a look that is still worn today. Even then, she knew she would be a couturiere for the ages. "Chanel is a style," she proclaimed. "Fashion goes out of fashion. Style never does."

COCO CHANEL

Chanel (in 1954) was famous also for pearls of wisdom. Regarding accessories: "Always remove things. Never put them back."

"Luxury must be comfortable; otherwise it is not luxury"

In 1957 (above), Chanel was 74, yet *The New Yorker* wrote that the designer had "the unquenchable vitality of a 20-year-old."

"A woman is trained into the suit; she doesn't just wear it," said Isaac Mizrahi. In '26 (left), Chanel modeled an early version.

George Bernard Shaw called Chanel (right, in 1929) "the fashion wonder of the world" and compared her to Marie Curie.

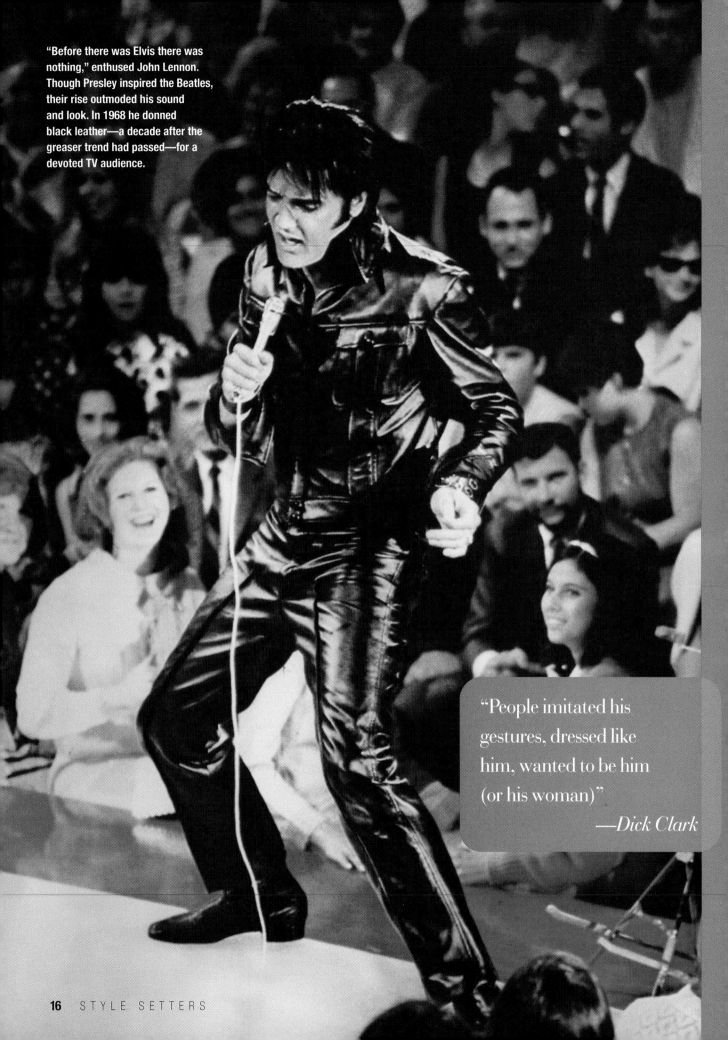

"Before there was Elvis there was nothing," enthused John Lennon. Though Presley inspired the Beatles, their rise outmoded his sound and look. In 1968 he donned black leather—a decade after the greaser trend had passed—for a devoted TV audience.

"People imitated his gestures, dressed like him, wanted to be him (or his woman)"

—*Dick Clark*

ELVIS PRESLEY

Long live the King—in song, but equally in ducktails, sideburns and those sequined jumpsuits

A young Presley tried out pink silk and eye shadow at the Grand Ole Opry. Fortunately he dropped those experiments for a sensible ducktail, which he reportedly spent hours perfecting.

As a poor kid in Memphis, Elvis Presley saved his dollars to shop on Beale Street, where black blues musicians found their look. It wasn't typical white teenage garb, but even then, Presley was dressing for the man he would become. After landing a contract with Sun Records, Elvis had a little pocket money and could really go to town. The scraggly pompadour became a sleek piece of architecture. The clothes, though tailored, were fluid enough to accommodate his swiveling hips in performance. By the time he hit Ed Sullivan's stage in 1956, he was a sight to behold; too bad CBS censors allowed him to be shot only from the waist up. The pinnacle of early Elvis fabulosity came the following year, when he purchased a $10,000 gold suit designed by Nudie, an ex-boxer who'd costumed burlesque dancers. (It appeared in multiple images on the cover of *Fifty Million Elvis Fans Can't Be Wrong*.) From that apex, he went over the top. Somewhere a rhinestone mine was stripped bare in order to bejewel giant capes, flared trousers and Presley's expanding waistband. The hair was now a helmet, the clothes a costume—one all too easily donned by impersonators for years to come.

"You need to apply more makeup around your eyes. They're too plain naturally. I like a lot of makeup," Presley instructed his bride, Priscilla Beaulieu. She followed orders on their wedding day in 1967.

"He liked pinks and blacks in the '50s," recalled a Memphis clothier, who sold Elvis more as fans tore his clothes.

Gaudy, yes, but don't you wish you had this Elvis look? In 1999 a rhinestone cape sold for $85,000, a jumpsuit for $65,000.

Stone debuted memorably at Cannes (above, in 1994) with Emanuel Ungaro's sunflowers. "Hers is the style of a big star," said Valentino. Stone proved it in 2000 (right). The whimsical star swiped her hubby's shirt (top), wrinkles and all, for the 1998 Oscars. "I was never much of an ironer," she explained.

When Sharon Stone and Vera Wang get a notion into their heads, it's as if they consider themselves fashion's Wright brothers. "We don't always get off the ground," explained Stone. "But when we do it's a big deal." Among their flights of fancy was the pairing of a white shirt belonging to her husband, San Francisco *Examiner* editor Phil Bronstein, with a Wang-designed lilac sarong (left). Although Wang is one of the actress's favorite designers, she isn't exclusive. "I wear what I like," she once said. And she has—even before she was a superstar with a wallet to match. As a newcomer to New York, she would attend friends' parties wearing men's silk pajamas with ladylike shoes. When she did finally make it—her breakthrough came at the advanced Hollywood age of 34, with *Basic Instinct*—she hadn't lost that eclectic sense of whimsy. At the 1996 Oscars she caused a stir by topping a long Valentino skirt with giant diamond cluster earrings from Van Cleef & Arpels and a Gap turtleneck. By projecting the fantasy of what a movie star should look like, Stone was living out her own childhood dreams. As a child in rural Pennsylvania, Stone has said, she made a big deal of watching movies from the '30s and '40s on TV, first preparing a tray of Ritz crackers and cheese canapés, then tuning in and taking note of what everyone wore: "Fred Astaire and Ginger Rogers were *it* for me." Stone would grow up to be the actress credited with returning early film grandeur to the red carpet, as exemplified in 1993 by a black beaded 1930s-style Valentino gown. Onscreen, however, Stone rarely gets to wear the classics she adores. *Basic Instinct* had her in a distracting white minidress and little else. Her Oscar-nominated turn in 1995's *Casino* outfitted her in 1970s Vegas call-girl gear. And the 1998 underwater thriller *Sphere* put her and Dustin Hoffman in matching submarine crew duds. That least-glamorous role taught Stone a valuable lesson. "Never do a movie," she joked, "where the boys and girls get the same costumes."

> "My personal style and public style are very different. When I go out, I play dress-up"

SHARON STONE

A student of '30s Hollywood glamour became a modern-day fashion original

She made the paparazzi's day in a sparkly-bodiced Valentino at Cannes in 1995.

A style influence on Stone (in 1999) was her grandma, a "tough lady in a fantastic Schiaparelli suit."

At the *101 Dalmations* premiere, she looked like Cruella de Vil, with puppy-friendly faux fur.

At an opening in '96, she was comfortable in a sweater set and gown.

Stone took a risk with a bold print at a Christie's benefit auction in 2000.

Bronzed (at the 1994 Comedy awards) or smiling (with Bronstein at the 1999 Golden Globes) or pretty in pink (at the 1999 premiere of *The Muse*), Stone loves to dress up. An AIDS philanthropist, she once said at a fund-raiser, "I'd sell the clothes off my back for AmFar. But maybe not tonight. I'm over 40." She's now 43.

SHARON STONE

"I don't have the calling to be a pincushion," Baker (in costume, 1951) once complained during a fitting.

Before there was J-Lo, there was Baker, who possessed the 20th century's most significant posterior. "The rear end exists," she once stated. "I see no reason to be ashamed of it." By leaving America and its prejudices, Baker created a sensation that shook all of Europe in the 1920s. "Her magnificent dark body," said one observer, "was a new model that, to the French, proved for the first time that black was beautiful." She gave them ample opportunity, dancing her African-inspired Charleston at the Folies Bergère in nothing but a skirt made of fake bananas. Soon Josephine dolls (complete with fruit) were sold throughout Paris. In her native St. Louis, her skin had been a liability; in France, cosmetics companies sold creams that promised a complexion like Baker's. Only after she had conquered Europe did American bookers suddenly demand Baker. Fully aware of her new clout, she furthered the redress of racism by refusing to perform in the States, except at desegregated clubs.

JOSEPHINE BAKER

...ual dancing ...made her a star, ...ocean away from ...homeland tha... wouldn't have he...

His short career left a legacy
of how to dress, how to walk
and how to pout like a rebel

Capturing Dean in a
biopic has proved
difficult. "If you do a
James Dean imitation,
they'll kill you," said
actor Ethan Hawke. "If
you don't do a James Dean
imitation, they'll kill you."

Had anyone ever worn blue jeans before? Not that you'd remember. They'd been around since the Gold Rush, but no one had taken much notice until they wrapped around a young man from Indiana, who jammed his hands in his pockets as he struck a defiant slouch under a red jacket, or stretched out in a convertible parked in front of a Texas ranch or hung his arms over a rifle as if it were a crucifix. Maybe Brando did the juvenile-delinquent pose first, but Dean wore it as comfortably as—well, as a pair of broken-in blue jeans. The famous red jacket belonged to Jim Stark of *Rebel Without a Cause*, the convertible to Cal Trask of *East of Eden* and the rifle to Jett Rink of *Giant*. But in this trilogy of angry-young-man films, there was no question that viewers were actually seeing Dean in all his own charismatic anguish. Had he lived past 24, he may have eventually outgrown the jeans and the scowl. As it is, he is frozen in 1955. As his *Rebel* costar Dennis Hopper said, "He was pure gold. The image he created [is] as contemporary today as then." And young rebels still wear blue jeans.

The actor had originally planned to wear his glasses in *Rebel,* but the idea was chucked when director Nicholas Ray chose color film and felt the specs clashed with Dean's red jacket.

"If Brando changed the way people acted," said Martin Sheen, "Dean changed the way people lived." (All photographs on these pages were taken in 1955.)

On September 30, 1955, Dean, then 24, showed off his new Porsche Spyder. Within hours, he would be killed in a collision with an oncoming car on a rural California road.

GRACE KELLY

A patrician beauty transformed herself from Hollywood royalty to the real thing

"Boy, was I crushed"
—*Oleg Cassini, whom Kelly dumped to marry Prince Rainier*

Alfred Hitchcock called her type Snow Princesses—frosty beauties who, paired with the right male costar and script, would become "snow-covered volcanoes." The former Philadelphia debutante proved his theory in *Dial M for Murder, Rear Window* and *To Catch a Thief*. The Princess found her Prince Charming, Rainier of Monaco, during the 1954 Cannes festival, after an introduction by matchmaking magazine editors. The couple married in 1956, giving the Oscar winner a new and appropriate title: Her Serene Highness. The wedding —and its elaborate preparations, including much-photographed shopping excursions in New York City—was central to the media fairy tale. (Years later, Kelly said that that image struck her as "rather icky and revolting.") Still, she dressed the part in a bridal gown by Hollywood designer Helen Rose. The paparazzi returned when the princess came home to shop for a layette, shortly after the honeymoon. She hid her pregnant belly behind a Hermès pocketbook, still known today as the Kelly bag. Though the world remembers her as the Princess Bride, intimates hold another view. "She was loads of fun," said her brother John, an Olympic rowing champ, "when she wasn't on display."

In 1982, Cheryl Ladd played Kelly (right, in '54) in a TV film. "When I was a young actress, I was never pretty or cute," said Kelly, somewhat blindly. But Cheryl "is both."

To get out of her contract with MGM, Kelly allowed the studio to film her 1956 wedding. Her dress was antique Brussels lace embroidered with pearls.

"She's still everywhere," said Rainier after her death in 1982. Indeed, she's in the faces— and the confident styles—of granddaughter Charlotte and daughter Caroline (in 2000).

25

"I would feel totally comfortable wearing Armani with army-navy"

Hill (this page and near right in 1998) is "positive, detailed, conscientious," said fan and collaborator Aretha Franklin. "I was surprised to see that in such a young woman. [She] is an old soul." Not so old, though, that she doesn't occasionally drop the glamour-girl look for pigtails and sweats (far right, onstage in Las Vegas).

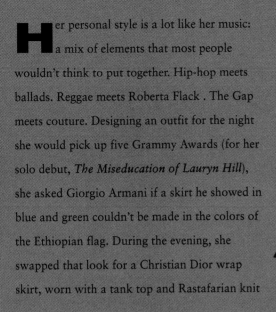

H er personal style is a lot like her music: a mix of elements that most people wouldn't think to put together. Hip-hop meets ballads. Reggae meets Roberta Flack . The Gap meets couture. Designing an outfit for the night she would pick up five Grammy Awards (for her solo debut, *The Miseducation of Lauryn Hill*), she asked Giorgio Armani if a skirt he showed in blue and green couldn't be made in the colors of the Ethiopian flag. During the evening, she swapped that look for a Christian Dior wrap skirt, worn with a tank top and Rastafarian knit

At the 1999 Grammy awards, she show-cased Armani, a hoard of gold and a genuine smile.

LAURYN HILL

A mix-master minx samples from her roots, runways and the mall

cap. "The way I put things together," she has said, "it's a little part rugged, a little part rootsy, but it also can get high fashion sometimes." Though her tours have been sponsored by Levi's, which dressed her onstage, she hardly qualifies as a poster girl for cookie-cutter clothing, gravitating instead to one-of-a-kind pieces. Whoopi Goldberg, who gave a then-unknown Hill a bit part in *Sister Act 2,* is a fan of the mix. "Lauryn," she says, "is sublime."

Marlene
Dietrich

The German expatriate seduced Hollywood with a sensual duality never before seen in a leading lady or man

Her masculinity appeals to women, and her sexuality to men," wrote critic Kenneth Tynan of film's reigning androgynous diva, the star of *Blue Angel, Shanghai Express* and *Witness for the Prosecution*. But though the Berliner popularized men's suits on women, she was no drag queen. She showed up once for the Academy Awards in a Dior gown so revealing that the producers hired a censor to monitor her onstage. That Dietrich could successfully pull off either look is a testament to both her attitude—and her architecture. She herself felt that the former was far more important. "Darling, the legs aren't so beautiful—I just know what to do with them," she once said. Indeed she did. A parade of her lovers, from John Wayne to Edith Piaf, could likely attest to that. Her romantic conquests were as much a part of Dietrich's legend as her arched brows. Once, gazing into the mirror before a cabaret performance, she remarked, "Look at her. Frightening, isn't it?" She toured well into her 70s, submerging herself in feathers, sequins and beads. Looking 30 years younger, she remained a master of the glamorous illusion.

"She spent an enormous amount on clothes," recalled grandson Peter Riva of Dietrich (left, in 1955). "She believed they were part of her image." One acquisition: an $8,000 white swansdown coat.

"I'm sure a man would do a far better impersonation than I could"
—*Sian Phillips, who played Dietrich onstage*

"Shoes are more important than suits and dresses," said Dietrich (above, on the Paramount lot in 1933). "Buy one pair of good shoes instead of three pairs of bad quality."

"I'm told she would stand for six hours for a fitting, determining where each sequin would be placed," said Sian Phillips of Dietrich (left, ca. 1942). "That obsessiveness is part of her character."

By following her own change-your-life prescription, a talk diva made herself over

Although Oprah Winfrey is among the richest women in the country, her closet probably looks a lot like any other gal's. On one side, there's a collection of loose-fitting clothes bought when her weight was at a peak (245 pounds) and, at the other end, a few sleek numbers held on to in the hope that she'll fit into them once again (size 8 was her smallest). On her eponymous talk show, a Nielsen champ since 1986, Winfrey has shared her weight roller coaster with an audience of millions, most of whom nod appreciatively as she testifies to the trouble with dieting. Having secured her everywoman status, Winfrey eventually found a healthy path to relative svelteness, though one hardly available to the masses: She works out religiously with a personal trainer, and retains a home chef to prepare low-fat meals. In 2000, a woman who once silently prayed that she would lose to Phil Donahue at the Emmy Awards, so that she wouldn't have the cameras follow her up to the podium (she won), became the confident cover girl of her own magazine. On one issue she modeled a red taffeta gown by Gianfranco Ferré. As with the novels plugged by her book club, public demand for the dress was enormous. Wearing beautiful, well-fitted clothes is clearly now a pleasure for Winfrey. But her fans don't see her real favorites: "Pajamas! That's my thing. I *love* pajamas."

At her heaviest, Oprah (above, '86) put aside a pair of size 10 Calvin Klein jeans. If they fit, "I thought my whole life would be okay."

With its devoted following and cultural clout, Oprah's show was a mandatory Bush campaign stop in 2000.

Oprah's own changeover began in '94, when she ditched sensationalism for motivational themes. In '95 (right) she was honored by *Essence*.

O readers won't find diet tips, as in other women's mags. But the editor (in '01) told them where to buy her favorite silk jammies.

OPRAH WINFREY

Winfrey (in '96) said the turning point came when she made a 1990 worst-dressed list, alongside Marge Simpson, in a gown "I thought I looked pretty decent in."

"I loved looking good, but needed people to tell me. I had [a] self-esteem problem"

"I was born at the right time for the thing I turned into —this new kind of woman who wanted to wear pants"

KATHARINE HEPBURN

Defying trends in favor of what was comfortable, this practical New Englander inadvertently made trousers as glamorous as ball gowns

"Can you imagine winning a fashion award for not giving a damn about clothes?" she chuckled in 1985, when the Council of Fashion Designers of America honored Hepburn with a lifetime achievement award. Tastemaking was the last thing on her mind. "I wore pants because it was good sense," she reflected at age 87. "Other women will follow if it makes good sense, and someone else shows the way." (By then she hadn't worn a skirt in 20 years—and no longer even owned one. When men would tell her they preferred women in skirts, she retorted, "Try one.") In the '30s and '40s, Hepburn showed the way to elegant, egalitarian dressing onscreen. "I was never too interested in style," she maintained. "I was just interested in comfort." But Hepburn's pants were a fashion statement and a veritable declaration of independence. They made her the equal of her costars (frequently her offscreen love, Spencer Tracy) and signaled that she was to be taken seriously. Though nominated eight times and victorious four, she attended the Oscars only once, in 1974, to present an award to a friend. On that occasion she wore gardening clothes. Producers were furious. It wasn't as if she didn't look good in a gown. From her 1932 debut in *A Bill of Divorcement*, most of her roles called for at least one glamorous turn. And though she hated them—to her, stockings were "the devil's invention"—she carried them off convincingly, with her gorgeous, slender line and her face lit up by soaring cheekbones. A natural athlete who favored tennis, golf and swimming, she found a character in 1952's *Pat and Mike* that most closely matched her offstage personality. Her most daring role, she said, was onstage, playing Coco Chanel.

"I was sort of the New Woman at a very early point," said Hepburn (here in 1938).

Before they were lovers, Tracy (in 1948) described her as having "ambiguous sexuality."

Hepburn said that, were she a man, she wouldn't want a wife like herself. "I'd prefer someone sweet, who was a good cook."

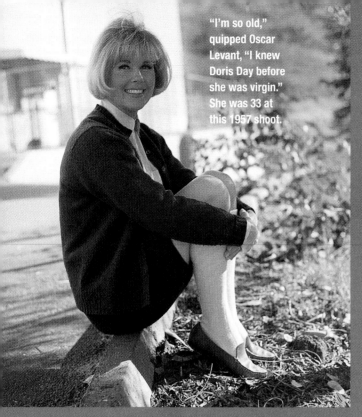

"I'm so old," quipped Oscar Levant, "I knew Doris Day before she was virgin." She was 33 at this 1957 shoot.

DORIS DAY

Wholesome and fresh as milk, her image charmed women as it intoxicated men

As a romantic conquest, she posed a challenge. So prim, so naive—what was she doing in those double-entendre sex farces with Cary Grant? And how would her onscreen suitors eventually get past that nice-girl exterior and win her over? An unimpressed critic called her cinema's "oldest living virgin," but audiences voted the perky blonde the favorite box office star three times between 1956 and 1962. Bandleader Les Brown, with whom she sang before launching her film career, recognized her appeal when Doris von Kappelhoff (as she was born in 1924 in Cincinnati) was just a teenager. "She had that pertness," he remembered. "That fresh look. I can't explain it, but it worked." Also hard to fathom: how a 33-year-old woman got away with knee socks and a pageboy. But the Ivory Snow image worked for her, even when she played against type, for instance in Alfred Hitchcock's *The Man Who Knew Too Much*. But Day wasn't willing to abandon entirely the good girl. In 1967 she turned down the part of the seductress in *The Graduate* (the role Anne Bancroft made her own). Though she headlined a TV sitcom for five more years, Day retired from film in '61, saying, "I want people to remember me the way I was."

In 1959 Day chilled on the *Pillow Talk* set with Rock Hudson, her three-time costar. Day (right, in *Pajama Game*, 1956) was as dedicated to that screen pairing as she was to costumer Jean-Louis, who clothed four Day pictures.

"It's a good thing I was married when we made those pictures," said James Garner of his costar (in 1957). "Otherwise I might have gotten into a lot of trouble."

"I had become . . . the woman men want to go to bed with, but not until they marry her"

"She's been a top model for well over a decade, and that's no small feat in a business where the flavor of the month may not even last a week"
—anchor Paula Zahn

Crawford (in 1990) generously credits all the "professional people" behind her in every photo shoot. "It's, like, I don't even look like Cindy Crawford sometimes."

Gorgeous, smart and charismatic, she projects a healthy image women relate to

CINDY CRAWFORD

There are models. There are supermodels (see pages 92–95). And then there is Cindy Crawford. For more than a decade, her penetrating gaze and dynamic smile, dotted by that famous mole, have graced the covers of some 440 magazines, setting the gold standard for all-American style and beauty. As an entrepreneur, pitchwoman, fashion columnist, exercise video guru and former hostess of MTV's *House of Style,* the hardworking Crawford has amounted to far more than the sum of those famously fabulous parts. When there were questions about her being cast as a lawyer in her 1995 movie debut *Fair Game,* she responded, "I was valedictorian of my high school, and I'm definitely smart enough." But she never lost perspective on her calling. "Fashion and style is just that," she has said. "Fashion and style. It's not brain surgery."

DIANA ROSS

Stop, in the name of love? Now in her fifth decade at the top, nothing stops the Supreme of Supremes

In 1961, the year the *other* Diana was born, *this* Diana cut her first single with the Supremes. Since then, Diana Ross has made so many albums (more than 60 to date), lent her sleek curves to so many gowns (last year in one show alone, she made 11 costume changes) and stayed so steadily in the spotlight that it is hard to imagine the zeitgeist without her. In the '60s, her Motown glam was hip but demure. After 1972's *Lady Sings the Blues* earned Oscar nominations for Ross and Bob Mackie, she went slinky. Bodysuits showed off her toned muscles during the exercise-crazed '80s. But it was her '90s turn toward the drama of Dolce & Gabbana that finally allowed Ross's inner and outer divas to sing in harmony.

> "She's ageless. She's the diva to end all divas"
> —*Vera Wang*

Ross (with Supremes Cindy Birdsong, left, and Mary Wilson in the mid-'60s) was voted Best Dressed in high school.

"Every time I call, my dad says, 'Hi, gorgeous!' That makes me feel beautiful"

JENNIFER LOPEZ

Let's consider that notorious awards gown just an asterisk on the record of a bountiful talent

Lopez (in '98) "wants to come up with new things," said her stylist Oribe. Among her novel looks: false eyelashes, made from red fox fur, at the 2001 Oscars.

Lopez was a star, both in film and on record, before The Dress. That fact may make all the difference when pop historians assess her career decades from now. Had she been an unknown when she slipped into that green Versace gown—which appeared to be no more than two scarves fastened with a brooch at her bikini line—then Lopez might well be remembered as the girl who got famous for dressing outrageously at the 2000 Grammy Awards. But no, there are other aspects to Lopez. She's the highest-paid Latina in Hollywood history, and in 2001 became the first person to have the country's No. 1 album (*J.Lo*) and No. 1 film (*The Wedding Planner*) in the same week. Still, people will continue to talk about that neck with the plunging neckline, the soaring slit, and the mystery of what kept it on. One upside: So long as they are reviewing The Dress's place in red-carpet history, they aren't going on about Lopez's earlier claim to style fame: her unwaifishly curvy behind. "I'm tired of talking about it," said an exasperated Lopez, but not before acknowledging the role of her often tightly wrapped derriere. "For so long [the style] was just skinny, skinny, skinny. I'm glad to contribute to the self-esteem of others." As for consigning The Dress to memory, she did turn up at the 2001 Oscars in a modestly tailored long skirt—and see-through top.

"She can pull anything off," cheered Randolph Duke of Lopez (singing in Switzerland, 2000).

"She thanks God that he made her the way she is," noted fitness guru Radu Teodorescu of Lopez (onstage in '99.)

The singer-actress (right, in 1997) added designer to her résumé in 2001, when she launched a J. Lo clothing line.

Never let 'em see you sweat. If Astaire had been an adman, he might have penned that pitch. His own technique for looking icebox cool when dancing? Layer long johns under your tux to absorb the perspiration. The physical embodiment of a Gershwin tune or a Cole Porter lyric, Astaire worked hard at making elegance look effortless. In fact it was hard work, and while he loved the dancing, he was less fond of the formalwear in which the public came to expect him. In close-up, Astaire lacked a movie idol's face, but he nonetheless seduced audiences with musical love scenes, waltzing across the screen with his partner in 10 films, Ginger Rogers. He could move just as suavely with a cane, a mop or a chair. "No dancer can watch Fred Astaire," said Mikhail Baryshnikov, "and not know that we all should have been in another business."

Pals like Jimmy Cagney saw past the Astaire aura (here, in 1951's *Royal Wedding*). "You know, you so-and-so," Cagney told him, "you've got a little of the hoodlum in you."

A Nebraska native tapped and twirled to become America's icon of urbanity

FRED ASTAIRE

Street-fighting man, or one of
wealth and taste, he defined
rock stardom devilishly

MICK JAGGER

He's a lovely bunch of guys,"
jibed his partner in rock,
Keith Richards. The guitarist was
referring to Jagger's mercurial
personality, but in four decades of
glory and notoriety, Jagger has
shown several sartorial personae as
well. The schoolboy who collared
his bad side in uniforms to match
his bandmates. The caped demon
who crooned for "Sympathy for the
Devil." The dandy rogue who epit-
omized an international lifestyle,
with homes, ex-wives and offspring
around the globe. The fit-at-40
rocker who took the stage in the
'80s wearing ill-advised football
pants. And now, the grandfather
(both of blues-infused rock and of
daughter Jade's two kids) who
refuses to hang up the microphone.
"People see more in me than there
is," Jagger once observed. "Yeah,
I've got layers. So does an onion."

"If you don't have that
energy, that libido, it's not
rock and roll anymore. It
becomes oldies music"

MARILYN MONROE

Her hair was bleached, the nose clipped, the mole penciled in. But this star's natural magic transcended the artifice

Monroe (in the mid-'40s) loved makeup even as a teen. "My arrival in school with painted lips and darkened brows started everyone buzzing," she recalled. "Why I was a siren, I hadn't the faintest idea."

"Sexuality is only attractive when it's spontaneous. This is where a lot of them miss the boat"

She is as notable first for what she didn't wear as for what she did. *Playboy*'s inaugural centerfold claimed to be more comfortable undressed than clothed. (Perhaps that was due to her habit of buying clothes a size too small to better show off her curves.) Despite her distaste for dressing, the former Norma Jeane Baker racked up a number of memorable looks in the sad short 12 years that she was Marilyn Monroe. Among them, the white halter dress that studio wardrober William Travilla created for 1955's *The Seven Year Itch*. Or the flesh-colored silk soufflé gown Jean Louis designed with more than 6,000 beads, which she wore while crooning "Happy Birthday" to President Kennedy in 1962. (A concession to her penchant for nudity: "It was impossible to wear undergarments with this dress," noted a curator at Christie's.) Monroe was also among the first female stars photographed in blue jeans, proving that she didn't need all that finery to look sexy. Just the crooked smile, the bed-tousled blonde hair, and a mystical appeal that starlets ever since have tried, and failed, to re-create.

The former Norma Jeane could turn on the Marilyn image like a light switch. "Wanna see me be 'her'?" she asked friends.

"Her derriere looked like two puppies fighting under a silk sheet," a critic once wrote of Monroe (right, in Korea in '54.)

Told she wasn't the star of *Gentlemen Prefer Blondes,* Monroe (in '55) replied, "Well, whatever I am, I am the blonde."

"If I'm going to be a symbol," said Monroe (in 1956), "I'd rather have it be [of] sex than some other things they've got symbols of."

THE BEATLES

Up to their moptops in fab gear,
the foursome presented an
awesome, artfully united front

Loved in London (in 1964), the Beatles wondered how they'd fare in the U.S. "They've got everything over there," said Harrison. "What do they want *us* for?"

"Visually, they are a nightmare," complained the New York *Daily News* the morning after the Beatles' seismic *Ed Sullivan* appearance in '64. The tabloid was particularly offended by their "tight, dandified Edwardian beatnik suits and great pudding bowls of hair." Though far shorter than what followed by decade's end, their long, combed forward coifs stirred controversy among the squares, while freeing America's young men to grow mop-tops (or don ankle-high Beatle boots). When they enlisted in Sgt. Pepper's Lonely Hearts Club Band, all four grew mustaches. But by 1965, uniform dressing was out, though they maintained a consistency of style. In India, they adopted beads and local garb. Then they went psychedelic, favoring paisley prints or stripes. When John Lennon tarted up in a green flowered shirt, red trousers and a Scottish sporran for his loose change, he didn't look out of place with the other three. Eventually, locks and facial hair became a free-for-all, and their matching collarless suits, neckties, turtlenecks and Nehru jackets were dispatched to the attics. At the group's final concert on a London rooftop in 1969, each man wore his own clothes (George Harrison, memorably, a fur coat and lime corduroys), signaling, sadly, that the Beatles would soon go their separate ways.

Their novel style (by Pierre Cardin, 1965) raised the question "Are you mods or rockers?" Neither, replied Ringo. "I'm a mocker."

The *Sgt. Pepper* sessions (1967), said maestro Leonard Bernstein, "inflame[d] my senses and sensibilities."

Their last photo shoot—and sartorial statement—was at Lennon's home in 1970.

"We looked like four Gene Vincents, or tried to" —*John Lennon*

"Not bad for a bunch of scruffs from Liverpool" —*Paul McCartney*

Angelic in earth tones, a young star emerged from a weepy flick with a much-imitated look

Playing Radcliffe coed Jenny Cavilleri in *Love Story*, a then-unknown MacGraw made famous the line "Love means never having to say you're sorry." Though it became the catchphrase of 1970, it wasn't nearly as ubiquitous as MacGraw's onscreen collegiate wardrobe. In the film, Harvard preppie Oliver Barrett gives up his inheritance to marry Jenny, so smitten is he with the girl in the maxi-length knit coats, knee-high leather boots and adorable crocheted cap. On the streets, women copied Jenny's look, no doubt jamming Kleenex in their knit pockets, after sitting through that tearjerker ending one too many times. MacGraw herself took the style offscreen by wearing a similar cap (left) to the 1971 Oscars, when she was nominated for Best Actress. A generation later, it came around again. Carolyn Bessette Kennedy greeted the press after her Aegean honeymoon in modern-day Jenny gear: a midi-length skirt and knee boots (page 49). More recently, designers Marc Jacobs and Tommy Hilfiger put the *Love Story* look on their runways. Oliver may never get over the loss of his love, but Jenny lives on in fashion.

ALI MACGRAW

"To me, that was the whole movie. Not the hospital scene, but the hat"
—*designer Isaac Mizrahi*

"People all over the world come up to me and tell me what the movie meant to them," said MacGraw (in 1970) 30 years after *Love Story*.

Woody Allen's muse
launched an endless trend:
Originality for everyone!

DIANE KEATON

Annie Hall is the model for how we dress in the last quarter of the 20th century," declared no less an authority than the Metropolitan Museum's costume curator, Richard Martin. "It is the basic template for Ralph Lauren and the Gap." It's true that, decades later, any woman can walk no further than the local mall to stock up on mannish Oxford shirts, chino pants and the occasional funky hat produced for the masses. But back in 1977, the look was brand-new and belonged solely to Keaton. (Though it did pay winking homage to Dietrich and Kate Hepburn, and seemed also to borrow heavily from the laundry hamper of a bachelor girl's apartment.) Keaton inspired then-boyfriend Woody Allen to write the title character, and later worked with costumer Ruth Morley to dress her. (Ralph Lauren was also consulted.) Paradoxically, though the clothes were meant to express Annie's quirky individuality, they soon turned up on millions of women, speaking as one in favor of the ensembles.

At the Oscars, *Annie Hall* took Best Picture, Best Actress for Keaton and Director for Allen. The costume award, however-er, went to *Star Wars*.

Diane (right, in 1978) doesn't take too much credit for the Hall phe-nomenon. Said she: "It was what was going on then. It was Downtown."

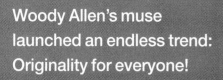

"She's one of those people you can put 400 things on, and she can make it all happen" —*costume designer Jeffrey Kurland*

JOHN AND CAROLYN KENNEDY

"They were teachers of how to live with grace, style, and being celebrities"
—Donna Karan

In a coup of secrecy, Kennedy and Bessette wed without press attention on South Carolina's Cumberland Island in 1996.

For a brief, shining moment, Camelot's second generation captivated a nation with great looks and inimitable style

My name is John Kennedy, and I am the man who is accompanying Carolyn Bessette to Milan," he told the press in 1997, echoing his father's wry comment on a 1961 presidential visit to Paris with his mother. Clever fellow. America's most photographed son knew that when he took up with Bessette, the media focus would be shared with this cool blonde who had captured the world's most eligible bachelor. A publicist for Calvin Klein when they met (a job she gave up when press questions about Kennedy outnumbered those about Klein), Bessette was soon looked on as a fashion heir to the late mother-in-law she never met. She began to live up to the title, for instance, at her 1996 wedding: Reversing a centuries-old trend of brides dressing like meringue desserts, she wore a sliplike column designed by Narciso Rodriguez. Though *Vogue, Bazaar* and every other magazine wanted her for their covers, Bessette Kennedy took

Updating an Ali MacGraw (page 46) look, Carolyn tromped New York with man and dog Friday in '98.

"He's gaga over her," said a Kennedy pal. Women were, too, and took to copying her sleek ponytails.

a Jackiesque approach to the press, which is to say she avoided it. (She also ignored John's example of complaining about the intrusive media even as he regularly paraded shirtless through Central Park.) When she was snapped by paparazzi, she was always meticulously turned out, whether in avant garde couture like Yohji Yamamoto at an anniversary party for her husband's magazine, or in smart jeans and a T-shirt to walk their dog. Tragically, the couple's status as style icons was solidified by a summer 1999 plane crash that ended their young lives. "John and Carolyn's joy for life, their elegance and composure in a world of intense scrutiny," said Giorgio Armani, "was a lesson for us all."

"She had a marvelous sense of quiet that permeated her entire look," said Mr. Blackwell of the new Mrs. Kennedy (in 1999).

TIGER WOODS

This golfer won't wear green, except at the Masters, but he redefines the color of money

Golf has a fuddy-duddy fashion history. Plus-four knickers. Argyle knee socks. Tam O'Shanters. When Tiger Woods turned pro in 1996 at age 21, he changed the game. First, he bested opponents and courses by unimaginable margins. Second, he was the sport's first African/Asian-American champion, turning a new multiethnic generation on to what had been a white man's pastime. And he dressed the part, putting the garish polyesters of the Arnold Palmer era in mothballs. In this department, he had some help from his pals at Nike, which signed him for a reported $150 million the year he went pro, and outfitted him in dignified, muted colors: charcoal, khaki, burgundy. "We start to talk about what [he'll wear] 18 months prior to the event," said a Nike rep. "The idea is to have the apparel in pro shops as soon as he models it." Whoosh. And ka-ching.

In fashion, Woods (in London in 2000) uses his business head: Getting a logo on the front panel of a golfer's hat can cost an advertiser $250,000 a year.

"He's Elvis. We've found Elvis, and he looks like Tiger Woods"

—*Rick Burton, a sports marketing authority*

MICHAEL JORDAN

His sports legend is sealed. But history
should not neglect his sartorial splendor

The confidence of a Sean Connery," swooned a female fan. "He's like Cary Grant," raved fashion tyrant Mr. Blackwell, "a very class act. From 1 to 10, I'd give him an 11." Said a grateful, head-shaved Damon Wayans: "He made being bald cool." Graceful on the court, his body soared into a logo-ready silhouette, the better to brand shoes and clothing with his stamp of cool aerodynamic athleticism. His Mr. Clean look would also help move cereal, batteries and undies, among other sundries. Elegant off the court, he led the league in custom-made suits from Milan. He was also responsible, in 1982, for making basketball's short-shorts obsolete, by asking for an extra inch on his uniform. The NBA's nattiest dresser also had a pretty fair slam dunk.

"He is, without a doubt,
in his way, the Duke
of Windsor"
—Mr. Blackwell

Jordan (above, in 1987, and left,
in 1994) learned more than
hoops at the University of North
Carolina. He credits coach Dean
Smith as also a fashion mentor.

NICOLE KIDMAN

The portrait of a lady, she wears her sensuality with fetching modesty—and a dash of humor

When seats to Broadway's *The Blue Room* started selling like winning lottery tickets, Nicole Kidman professed not to understand the fuss. "Suddenly, everybody focused on the nudity," she mused. "I was surprised at that." Make the 5'10" diaphanous stunner a party of one. Never mind that only her pale derriere was exposed—and only briefly at that. It was enough to sell out the 1998 run. Since bursting onto the Hollywood scene at 22, the freckle-faced sylph from Australia has let her natural beauty speak for itself. A slave to no couturier, she leads with her translucent skin, nimbus of red hair and impossibly long limbs. And why not. Whether she struts the red carpet Cruise-control-free in a clingy black gown or slums in a knee-brushing skirt and vintage sweater, the long-necked beauty has a to-die-for elegance that tends to upstage any design.

"I didn't sit down and go, 'Gosh, I want to be a prominent object of desire'"

DUKE ELLINGTON

A radiant smile and a penchant for sharp suits made the jazz maestro a glistening listen

Edward Kennedy Ellington's father had been a butler, a chauffeur and a caterer. And by patching together a decent wage from those jobs, he "lived like a man who had money," his son recalled. That included nurturing in his son a taste for fine clothes. Because of those dapper duds, young Edward had earned the school nickname Duke by age 12. His parents had encouraged him to take up piano at 7, with a teacher called Mrs. Clinkscales (true). By 19, he was making a living as a musician-for-hire in Washington, D.C. In his 20s, the Duke became the king of New York's night-clubs, launching a career that would produce some 2,000 compositions, including "Satin Doll" and "Mood Indigo." Always, he dressed to thrill: After seeing him at the Cotton Club, one woman couldn't remember the set list or who else played, but could clearly conjure the image of two purple velvet slippers stomping rhythmically under the piano.

"I was a pretty fancy guy"

Ellington (in New York in 1943) designed his own silk neckwear, dubbing them "kissy-poos."

53

MADONNA

Presto chango! The trampy vamp turned mommy-yogini is pop culture's premier provocateur

"When I'm 90 I'll be the Material Girl. It's not so bad; Lana Turner was the Sweater Girl till the day she died"

Corsets from the '90s "would never realistically have been picked up by a lot of people," noted museum costume curator Harold Koda. "But when she does it, it becomes inscribed on the cultural consciousness."

If necessity is the mother of invention, then Madonna is the mother of reinvention. For nearly two decades she has appropriated trends and repackaged them in a dramatically original way. She wasn't the first East Village club kid in the early '80s to wear ripped clothes and too many chains. Nor was she the first to vogue on the dance floor. Or to take up yoga and wear a bindi. Or to don cowboy duds ironically. Yet somehow it all seemed fresh when it emerged from the cultural Cuisinart that is Madonna. "Her eye is certainly right," cheered Karl Lagerfeld. Though she first played to concert halls filled with Madonna wanna-bes, sporting black lace and rubber bracelets, her later looks elicited interest if less imitation. (Not everyone can pull off the cone-bra conceit.) "I don't think she's of an age to launch a fashion trend," said designer Olivier Theyskens of the latter-day Madonna (though she helped establish him at a 1998 awards show). "It's better to launch a lifestyle trend, based on happiness. And she does that well." She certainly does. Fans who dropped off during the *Sex* book fiasco of 1992 are back to bask in the glow of the 43-year-old new-millennium Madonna: a wife, a mother of two and an honorary Londoner. Hey, she's not the first to feign an accent either.

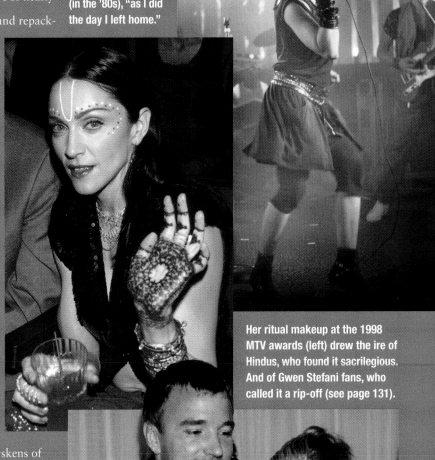

"I feel just as hungry today," said Madonna (in the '80s), "as I did the day I left home."

Her ritual makeup at the 1998 MTV awards (left) drew the ire of Hindus, who found it sacrilegious. And of Gwen Stefani fans, who called it a rip-off (see page 131).

White lace and crucifixes comprise the 1985 "Like a Virgin" getup. "Like" being the operative word.

Madge (as Britons call her) and Guy Ritchie took in a 2000 party, with son Rocco (under the dress).

BOY TOY

Vreeland (in 1983) was the model for the "Think Pink" editor in the 1957 film *Funny Face*.

She had no sitcom fizz, no movie-role magic, no rock-concert egomania with her image projected 50 feet high. What she did have, according to photographer Richard Avedon, a friend, was "the amazing gallop of her imagination." Between 1936 and 1971, first as editor of *Harper's Bazaar* and later of *Vogue*, Diana Vreeland was the premier diva of the fashion press. Vreeland practically invented the budget-busting exotic locale shoot, juxtaposing couture and ethnic costume. Each issue reflected the cultural kaleidoscope of her mind. For instance, a photo of hippies at Woodstock put her in mind of picnickers in a Seurat painting, so she ran the two images on facing pages. Her approval launched the careers of designers such as Diane von Furstenberg and Halston, photographers including Irving Penn and offbeat models like Lauren Hutton. Her pronouncements ("Pink is the navy blue of India") were legend. (Another quip: "Beware the legend.")

DIANA VREELAND

The woman who coined the term "the Beautiful People" was the mother of them all

Though she made some wild suggestions to readers ("Why don't you turn an old mink into a bathrobe?"), she was a conservative dresser who favored black and neutral fabrics in tailored suits. That uniform served as a canvas for her bold and plentiful jewelry, including omnipresent Chanel cuff bracelets. Then, the face. Rouge like a china doll. Poppy red on the mouth, the better to accentuate such bons mots as "A little bad taste is like a nice splash of paprika. What I object to is no taste."

"Fashion is not important, but one's appearance is important"

Can there be any greater accolade for a fashionista than being elected to the Fashion Hall of Fame after holding a place on the best-dressed list for 14 years? For Barbara "Babe" Paley, yes. In 1975, 18 years after her Hall of Fame induction, she was named Superdresser of Our Time by industry pollsters. "All the superlatives are true," raved fashion illustrator Kenneth Paul Bloch. Paley, briefly a *Vogue* editor in the 1940s, found her life's work as the wife of CBS founder and chairman William S. Paley. The job entailed being seen at the right events, playing the consummate hostess and dressing very, very well. Twinsets at the absolute right moment. A sheath dress that, for years after her death in 1978, people still referred to as the Babe. (The style reappeared in the early '90s.) To dress that well, one needed to possess two important qualities. Though Paley obviously had both, it is she who is credited with first saying, "You can never be too rich or too thin." You can, however, be too obsessive. Though her husband's millions could have financed a private laundry staff, Paley, trusting no one, washed her own shirts by hand.

She was, said one admirer, "perfection in an era of casual convenience." Here in 1965 she dined (lightly) with her husband at La Côte Basque in Manhattan.

BABE PALEY

CBS may have been the Tiffany network, but she was the real jewel in the crown of her mogul mate

"She had only one fault: She was perfect. Otherwise, she was perfect"
—*Truman Capote*

FRANK SINATRA

He wasn't a songwriter but a singer who turned his life and look into a composition. And what he did for a tune, he could do for a suit

"Francis, why do you need so many suits?" President Kennedy's father asked Sinatra, who once owned 150. The singer (in 1954) replied, "Why do you call me Francis?"

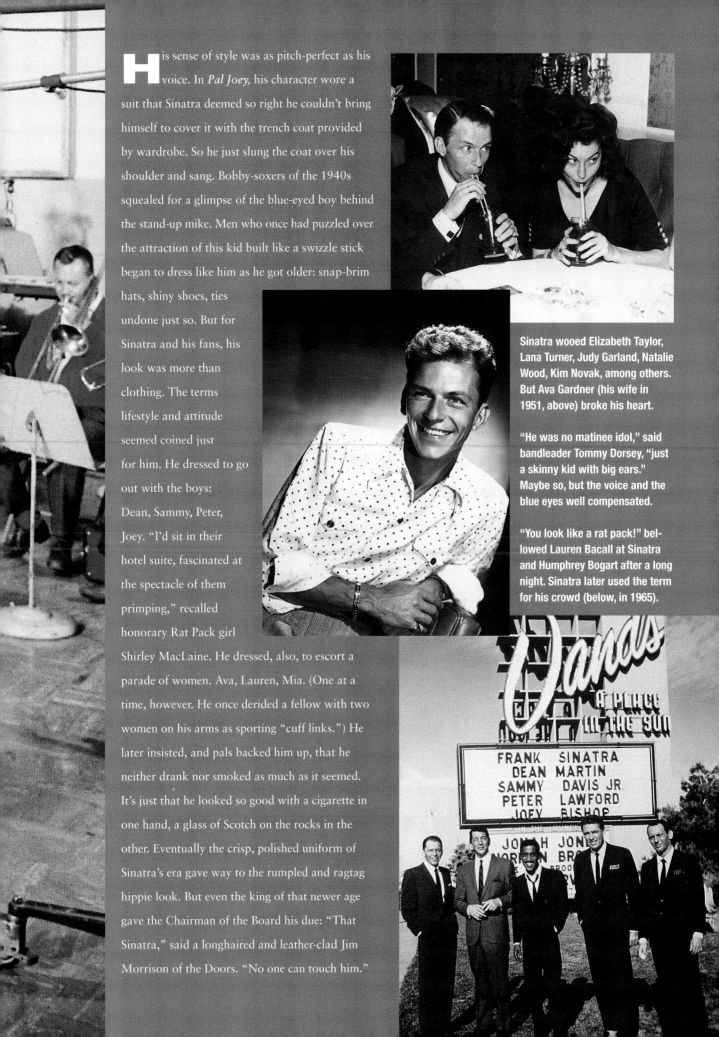

His sense of style was as pitch-perfect as his voice. In *Pal Joey,* his character wore a suit that Sinatra deemed so right he couldn't bring himself to cover it with the trench coat provided by wardrobe. So he just slung the coat over his shoulder and sang. Bobby-soxers of the 1940s squealed for a glimpse of the blue-eyed boy behind the stand-up mike. Men who once had puzzled over the attraction of this kid built like a swizzle stick began to dress like him as he got older: snap-brim hats, shiny shoes, ties undone just so. But for Sinatra and his fans, his look was more than clothing. The terms lifestyle and attitude seemed coined just for him. He dressed to go out with the boys: Dean, Sammy, Peter, Joey. "I'd sit in their hotel suite, fascinated at the spectacle of them primping," recalled honorary Rat Pack girl Shirley MacLaine. He dressed, also, to escort a parade of women. Ava, Lauren, Mia. (One at a time, however. He once derided a fellow with two women on his arms as sporting "cuff links.") He later insisted, and pals backed him up, that he neither drank nor smoked as much as it seemed. It's just that he looked so good with a cigarette in one hand, a glass of Scotch on the rocks in the other. Eventually the crisp, polished uniform of Sinatra's era gave way to the rumpled and ragtag hippie look. But even the king of that newer age gave the Chairman of the Board his due: "That Sinatra," said a longhaired and leather-clad Jim Morrison of the Doors. "No one can touch him."

Sinatra wooed Elizabeth Taylor, Lana Turner, Judy Garland, Natalie Wood, Kim Novak, among others. But Ava Gardner (his wife in 1951, above) broke his heart.

"He was no matinee idol," said bandleader Tommy Dorsey, "just a skinny kid with big ears." Maybe so, but the voice and the blue eyes well compensated.

"You look like a rat pack!" bellowed Lauren Bacall at Sinatra and Humphrey Bogart after a long night. Sinatra later used the term for his crowd (below, in 1965).

He was stepping into some big, bad-ass shoes. When Jackson was tapped to update the title role in *Shaft*, created in 1971 by Richard Roundtree, he knew he had to live up to the character and a theme song that boasted he was "a sex machine to all the chicks." Roundtree had attacked the part of the suave P.I. in funky leather blazers and flared pants. In 2000, Jackson sought help from Armani. "I'll design the clothes," the Italian master promised. "You'll create the attitude." The film's costumer rounded up other looks from Versace, Kenzo and Missoni. Offscreen, the 6'3" actor favors similar names. "I could be hanging out with gangsters or hanging out with diplomats and, by putting on Armani, maintain the air of class that either of those situations demands," Jackson once said. He also has a flair for creating his own trend, as he did by wearing a Kangol cap throughout *Jackie Brown*, and before paparazzi at public events. Now the look is so identified with Jackson that at his 50th birthday party, wife LaTanya told guests that if they wanted to find him, "just look for the Kangol, darling." Hardly blending into the crowd, the birthday boy greeted the big five-0 in a red velvet suit. Can you dig it?

"Sam has a prance in his step that brings clothing to life"
—*Giorgio Armani*

Jackson's ubiquitous cap turned up in '98 both on the golf course and at his 50th-birthday party, where guests got monogrammed versions as favors.

SAMUEL L. JACKSON

The Gene Hackman of his generation, he's a very busy chameleon onscreen, and a tiger dresser off

"Something I've never been, that I will never be, is hip," Zeta-Jones (at the '99 Oscars) has admitted.

With her sparkling eyes, womanly curves and regal sense of style, actress Zeta-Jones flaunts a saucy retro femininity that harkens back to the days of such legendary screen goddesses as Ava Gardner and Rita Hayworth. This Welsh rarebit, whose symmetrical features represent the alpha and omega of classical beauty, stops *Traffic* even on that most celebrated of runways, the Motion Picture Academy's red carpet. In 1999, her strapless red Versace gown and natural endowments nearly caused a photographer pileup as shutters popped their chorus of approval. Two years later, her black satin bustier gown, also by Versace, helped put boned corsets back on the fashion map.

CATHERINE ZETA-JONES

With a nod to screen beauties of yore, she puts the sigh back in siren

As someone who freely concedes, "I've worked hard at trying to look my best," Zeta-Jones burnishes her glam-puss image with all the tools at her disposal. A self-professed clotheshorse, she purposefully shuns hip street trends, instead draping herself in expensive designs by the likes of Chanel and Dolce & Gabbana. She is also unafraid to treat her face like a Rembrandt canvas, experimenting with liberal amounts of makeup from a palette that runs the full range of colors. "It's like painting to me," she has said. "I came out of the womb wearing makeup." Zeta-Jones, who self-admittedly "was never interested in being part of the pack," makes no apology for her celebrity, her A-list marriage to the 25-years-older Michael Douglas or her elegant tastes. Instead, with a self-aware wink at the incredible brightness of her being, she basks in her hard-won attention, exulting with refreshing candor, "I love being a woman."

> "I always said that old Hollywood was so lost . . . but Catherine proves otherwise"
> —*stylist Fati Parsia*

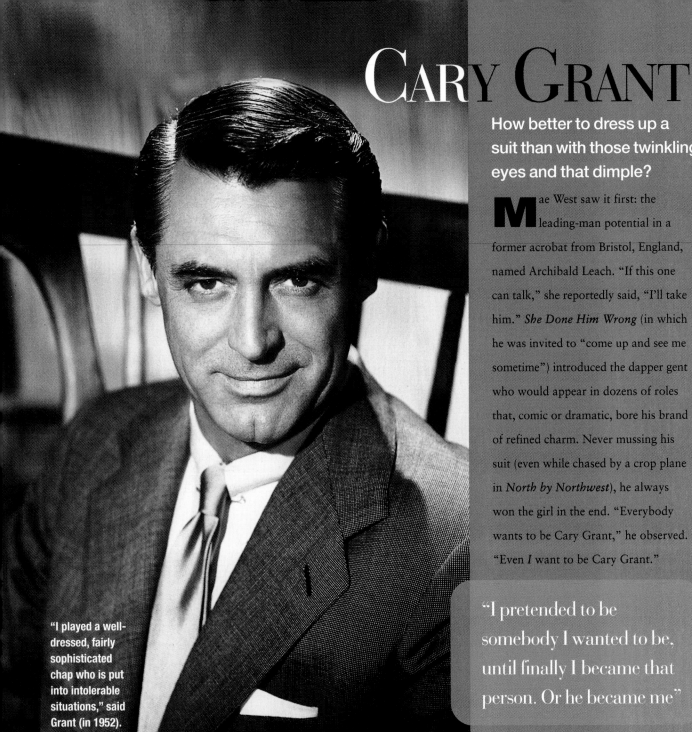

CARY GRANT

How better to dress up a suit than with those twinkling eyes and that dimple?

Mae West saw it first: the leading-man potential in a former acrobat from Bristol, England, named Archibald Leach. "If this one can talk," she reportedly said, "I'll take him." *She Done Him Wrong* (in which he was invited to "come up and see me sometime") introduced the dapper gent who would appear in dozens of roles that, comic or dramatic, bore his brand of refined charm. Never mussing his suit (even while chased by a crop plane in *North by Northwest*), he always won the girl in the end. "Everybody wants to be Cary Grant," he observed. "Even *I* want to be Cary Grant."

"I played a well-dressed, fairly sophisticated chap who is put into intolerable situations," said Grant (in 1952).

> "I pretended to be somebody I wanted to be, until finally I became that person. Or he became me"

Would the neckties, the gloves, the scarves, the jewels—let's not forget the jewels—be so enchanting were it not for the romance of the couple who wore them? Indeed. Famous for a courtship that caused the first voluntary abdication of the British throne, Edward VIII and Wallis Simpson were also a couple of royally great shoppers. Freed in 1936 from the responsibilities of being king

and queen, the Duke and Duchess of Windsor (so titled by Edward's younger brother, King George VI) enjoyed a life built around flitting from Paris to New York to Palm Beach, hunting and gathering as they went. (They often unloaded surpluses in informal trunk shows for friends.) The Duke's personal wardrobe changed menswear. He popularized more casual dress, mixing plaids and tweeds

with abandon and throwing a Saville Row jacket over the whole lot. Gents today owe him the zipper fly and, of course, the Windsor knot. Simpson, a tall, plain, twice-divorced Yank, flattered her boyish figure with bias-cut gowns, impeccably tailored suits and gobs of jewelry. The style and the romance were inextricable: Most anything gold or platinum they had inscribed to each other.

The 20th century's most romantic—and most scandalous—love story was also its best costumed

THE DUKE & DUCHESS OF WINDSOR

"Since I can't be pretty, I try to look sophisticated"
—*Wallis Simpson*

With her megawatt smile and can-do spirit, Britney Spears could be the girl-next-door. That is, if she weren't a pop-tart sensation worth millions who has made tube tops, glitter makeup and belly buttons must-see fashion accessories for the prepubescent crowd. Say what you will about the former Mouseketeer—and rest assured, critics have said it all—this is one icon who is adding a new chapter to the book on image control. To devoted wannabes, she offers onstage hugs and the prospect (albeit remote) of dropping in unannounced at their homes. To fans' parents, she offers a strong work ethic and a vow to remain a virgin until her wedding night. And to everyone else, she offers an ever-escalating tease. Her first video—a cooing Lolita-style number in which she ambiguously entreats viewers to "hit me, baby, one more time"—was shrewdly followed by a guest-host gig on *Saturday Night Live* that enabled her to lampoon her squeaky-clean image. Then, in September 2000, the 5'7" gamine stripped off her clothes at the MTV Video Music Awards to reveal a flesh-toned, skin-hugging halter top and pants—thus launching her perilous passage from bubblegum ingenue to full-fledged diva. Still, the vixenette isn't surrendering her virgin franchise quite yet. *A Mother's Gift,* the second book she's coauthored with Mom, recently hit the bestseller charts. Now, ain't that sweet?

On the road from naive teenybopper to savvy temptress, Spears (in 2000) said, "It's nice to feel sexy sometimes."

"I dress the way I want," she (left, in 2000) wrote in *Britney Spears' Heart to Heart.* "I don't pretend to be someone I'm not."

After Spears (in 2000) added a navel ring, a tattoo and cleavage, her comanager Larry Rudolph said, "She's totally in control of what's going on."

Britney Spears

No *Oops!* about it. With a canny blend of doe-eyed fawn and jailbait vamp, the pop singer keeps doing it again and again

Spears (in 2000) has a fan in fellow MTV star Sisqó. "Britney rocks," he cheers. "She's got the powers."

"People can copy her, but no one can match her emotion"
—*record producer Jimmy Jam*

Blige (in 1997) has said she now favors dressing up, whether performing or not. "But," she added, "I save the cleavage for onstage."

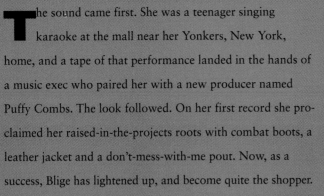

The sound came first. She was a teenager singing karaoke at the mall near her Yonkers, New York, home, and a tape of that performance landed in the hands of a music exec who paired her with a new producer named Puffy Combs. The look followed. On her first record she proclaimed her raised-in-the-projects roots with combat boots, a leather jacket and a don't-mess-with-me pout. Now, as a success, Blige has lightened up, and become quite the shopper. Versace. Fendi. Chanel. Gucci. (Turns out she always had a fondness for glamour: Her sister revealed in TIME that Blige is a closet Bette Davis fan.) Other signs of her transformation: On her most recent album, she teamed with clotheshorse Elton John for a duet. M.A.C cosmetics hired her to help move Viva Glam lipstick. And Dolce &

MARY J. BLIGE

Hip hop's tough girl traded in a gangsta look for a glam makeover

Gabbana sponsored her tour. "It was a natural transition," said Blige. "I never played dress-up as a child. I was more of a tomboy until I was 19. Now I'm a big fan of fashion, but I have my own style." Enough so that her look could be co-opted by comic book artist Stan Lee, who has cast Blige as his latest superhero.

"I've had the Farrah Fawcett feathers," said Blige (in 2000). "But everybody's doing them, so now I have to change."

In 2000 (left), Blige considered designing her own clothes, only to decide, "For now I'll wait and see."

Blige calls her hair (red, in '99) high-maintenance. "I'm always getting it woven, permed, cut or styled." Oh, and dyed.

Looking in '99 like the lost member of LaBelle, Blige, said MTV veejay Kennedy, "wants to give you a party every time she steps out of her closet."

KATIE COURIC

Smiling when the rest of us are still fumbling for the toothbrush, she starts America's day with refreshing normalcy

She rises at 5 a.m. At the saner hour of 7:00, when the bleary-eyed tune in to *Today*, she's smiling, and wide, wide awake. If they didn't love her so, that indomitable perkiness might grate. But they do love her. She's smart and quick but still girl-next-door. She gets excited. She asks questions that viewers believe they would ask. And she isn't a snob about her success. (Though fans realize that her predawn percolation has made her a mint.) Like them, she loves the Gap and did her own dye jobs. But in 2000 Couric seemed to go with her star status. She began wearing designers like Marc Jacobs and entrusting her hair to colorist Louis Lacari. Whatever fans thought, other anchors were relieved. Said one: "I'm glad Katie is stretching the limit."

"I can barely remember to put on deodorant in the morning"

JOAN COLLINS

**Forget that dame on CNBC: Alexis
Carrington was the primo money honey**

"Standards of style have
deteriorated. Coco Chanel
and Christian Dior must
be turning a paler shade
of pink in their graves"

The bitch image of Alexis somehow got blurred with mine," Collins once said, adding, "In a way, one can be complimented: If I'm totally confused with the character, I'm doing the character right." Another sign that the actress and her *Dynasty* alter ego might have merged: She was notorious for lugging more luggage through Heathrow Airport than any other VIPs except Elizabeth Taylor and Elton John. And playing a refugee from Nazi Germany who builds a fashion and publishing empire in *Sins,* she set a record for most costume changes (85) in a TV miniseries. How can you tell when a woman like that is out of her element? Rent the 2000 feature *The Flintstones in Viva Rock Vegas,* in which our Joan plays Fred's mother-in-law. "The costumes," she groaned, "were so unforgiving." Translation: No sequels until leopard-skin togas come with shoulder pads.

SARAH JESSICA PARKER

Like her TV alter ego, she knows her way around New York—and the racks at Barney's

"I have every pair of Manolo Blahniks I ever bought. I don't care if the heel is broken; they're art"

When she took the lead role in *Sex and the City,* Parker knew that viewers would tune in for the sex, but she didn't want them to forget the city. "I think the chic aesthetic that we see in New York is what separates women in this city from any other," she said. "And it's why I have been so dogmatic about the way women look on this show." The show's creative consultant as well as its star, Parker collaborates with costumer (and Manhattan boutique owner) Patricia Field to give her character, Carrie Bradshaw, and the three other women in her clique a very up-to-the-moment look. Fendi baguette bags, Manolo Blahnik heels, bare legs with skirts, so-tacky-they're-cool ID necklaces—all these trends have their roots in *City*'s style. "A lot of single women in their 30s tend to spend their disposable income on clothes," notes Candace Bushnell, author of the book on which the series is based. "That's one of the reasons all these fashion houses have just exploded." Although little about Bradshaw's life mirrors Parker's (the fictional sex columnist is a serial dater, while the Ohio-born actress is happily married to Matthew Broderick), the two women do share clothes. The flesh-colored Donna Karan minidress that seemed to disappear into Bradshaw's skin was actually pulled from Parker's closet. And on a visit to Conan O'Brian's couch, Parker borrowed a pair of Bradshaw's shorts. Why not? Both ladies, who are the same trim size 0, can wear anything.

"I could run a marathon in heels," said Parker (in 2000), so accustomed is she to the unforgiving height of her 100 pairs of Blahniks.

"They've become a new fashion authority," said *Bazaar* editor Kate Betts of the *City* cast. In 2000, Parker took a TV look to an awards show by sporting a giant corsage.

Adorning the 2000 Emmys with hubby Broderick, Parker joked of her Oscar de la Renta pink ostrich confection, "I have to be very careful. I think I'm flammable."

"I don't dress nearly as flashy as my character," said Parker (as Bradshaw in 1999). "But I have been influenced."

"After Farrah stopped wearing bras, the other girls followed"
—*Nolan Miller, their costume designer*

The original '76 lineup included Kate Jackson (Sabrina Duncan), Farrah Fawcett (Jill Munroe) and Jaclyn Smith (Kelly Garrett). In the Hollywood homage of 2000, Drew Barrymore, Cameron Diaz and Lucy Liu took over the Townsend Agency.

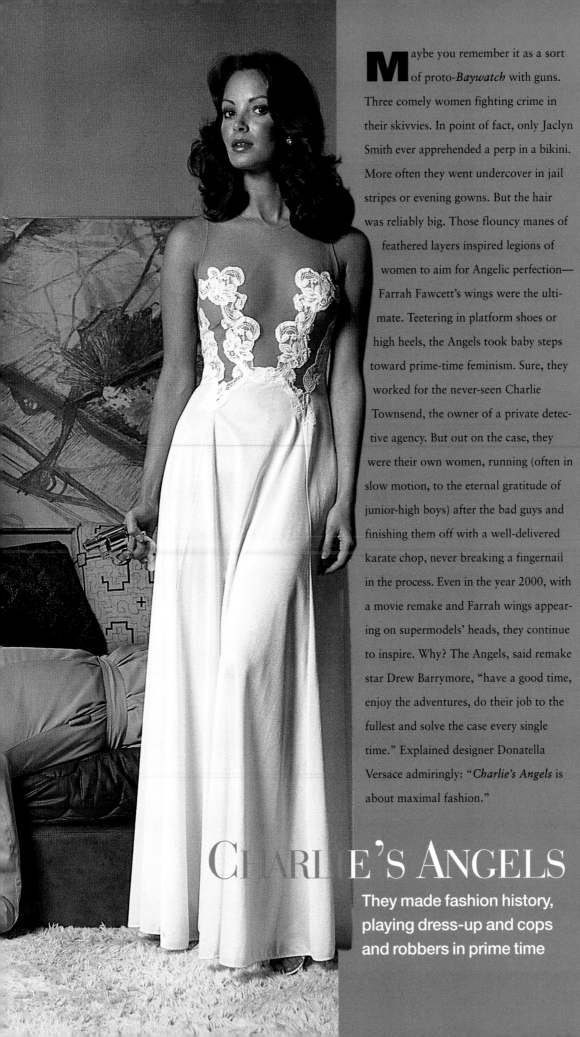

Maybe you remember it as a sort of proto-*Baywatch* with guns. Three comely women fighting crime in their skivvies. In point of fact, only Jaclyn Smith ever apprehended a perp in a bikini. More often they went undercover in jail stripes or evening gowns. But the hair was reliably big. Those flouncy manes of feathered layers inspired legions of women to aim for Angelic perfection— Farrah Fawcett's wings were the ultimate. Teetering in platform shoes or high heels, the Angels took baby steps toward prime-time feminism. Sure, they worked for the never-seen Charlie Townsend, the owner of a private detective agency. But out on the case, they were their own women, running (often in slow motion, to the eternal gratitude of junior-high boys) after the bad guys and finishing them off with a well-delivered karate chop, never breaking a fingernail in the process. Even in the year 2000, with a movie remake and Farrah wings appearing on supermodels' heads, they continue to inspire. Why? The Angels, said remake star Drew Barrymore, "have a good time, enjoy the adventures, do their job to the fullest and solve the case every single time." Explained designer Donatella Versace admiringly: "*Charlie's Angels* is about maximal fashion."

CHARLIE'S ANGELS

They made fashion history, playing dress-up and cops and robbers in prime time

CHER

She happily inhabits a
fashion fantasyland
where few would dare go

Designers Anna Sui,
Tom Ford and Dolce &
Gabbana call Cher (in
1985) an inspiration.

"It was just like
assembling a Rose
Parade float"
—Bob Mackie on a
Cher Oscar gown

Queen of the Nile, 1978

Pirate Wench, 1984

Indian Princess, 1979

Jewel Dripper, 1978

Fitness Buff, 1985

For her 1999 directing debut, Cher chose a TV film script called *If These Walls Could Talk*. (The walls were in a women's clinic.) Would that her closet walls could talk. They might reminisce about the bell-bottoms and fur vests that got a young Cher and husband Sonny Bono kicked out of a London hotel. They'd have a lot of dish on designer Bob Mackie, the person most attached to Cher's navel, save for her own mother. (They are a catty bunch, the walls.) Mackie, in collusion with Cher, was responsible for the preponderance of sequins, feathers and fringe—not to mention skin—on her two TV shows, in her Las Vegas acts and at awards ceremonies. The walls would recall the Indian phase, the dominatrix phase and the day they made room for exercise clothes, when Cher started shilling for Jack LaLanne. Oh, and that sheer leotard with the strategically placed leather V from the video for "If I Could Turn Back Time." In fact, she did, with three cosmetic surgeries before age 32. Still, the glitz queen's greatest feat was transforming herself into a serious actress; she won an Oscar for 1987's *Moonstruck*. As *The New York Times* noted, "When you take away those wild wigs, there's an honest, complex screen presence underneath." That's not much fun for the closet walls, but they can't disagree.

"He knew what was right for us," said Cher of Bono (in '72).

"She could wear anything," said Mackie, who made this 1998 ensemble.

See? She does have real clothes. Cher, fab at 54, in 2000.

"You're a hell of a
mover. Man, you
really put them on
their asses last night"
—*Fred Astaire, in a*
phone call to Jackson

MICHAEL JACKSON

At stadiums around
the world, his exultant
(and emulating) fans
offered up the sound
of one glove clapping

In military drag in the 1980s, Jacks
an unstoppable army of one. Havir
escaped from the ranks of the Jackson
decorated himself with more epaulets a
medals of honor than Patton. He conq
the pop charts with "Thriller" and mo
with a captivating appearance on the N
25th Anniversary TV special. That 198
saw Jackson hike up his black trousers
gloved hand to expose blinding white
and black loafers. As audience eyes ad
the loafers slid as if walking forward,
son, seemingly on air, glided backward
move dubbed the moonwalk. Unlike M
his only competitor for the '80s pop cr
Jackson did not reinvent himself with e
record. Instead, he remained encased in
regalia, and clung to that stray white g
(waving it even from the stretcher that
him away from a pyrotechnic accident
in the '90s, he ventured meekly into m
bondage gear: vinyl pants loaded with
Finally, in 2001, anticipating Jackson's
album in eight years, his record label n
a change and forced stylists to sign cor
agreeing not to dress Jackson in his ol
was time for the generalissimo to retir

He loved fame. His own, or other people's. As subjects for his canvases, he chose icons—Marilyn, Elizabeth, Jackie—who could be reduced to one name and a few swaths of color pressed through a silk screen. Not long after arriving from Pittsburgh to design shoes, Andy himself was a Manhattan icon. His platinum wig and trendsetting ensemble of blazer, white shirt, jeans and loafers sans socks became as recognizable as his soup-can paintings. By the '70s, museums were gobbling up his work, and he held court at Studio 54. Long before Madonna brought voguing from gay discos to MTV, Warhol had put the underground into the limelight. His camera eye saw a future where nothing is so fashionable as that which is commercially success-ful, and by his 1987 death saw it come to pass.

"It would be very glamorous to be reincarnated as a great big ring on Liz Taylor's finger"

"In the future, everyone will be famous for 15 minutes," he said in '67, the year after he shared the stage (right) with Edie Sedgwick and Chuck Klein.

Updating Dada, fashion and fame, this self-promoter became a papa of pop art

ANDY WARHOL

"I saw these pants and asked my friend, 'Are they tacky?' She said, 'Not if *you* wear them'"

Her dad later bought her the $160,000 Harry Winston choker she was lent for the '99 Oscars.

GWYNETH PALTROW

A Hollywood scion, of 1972 vintage, is a throwback to a more glamorous era

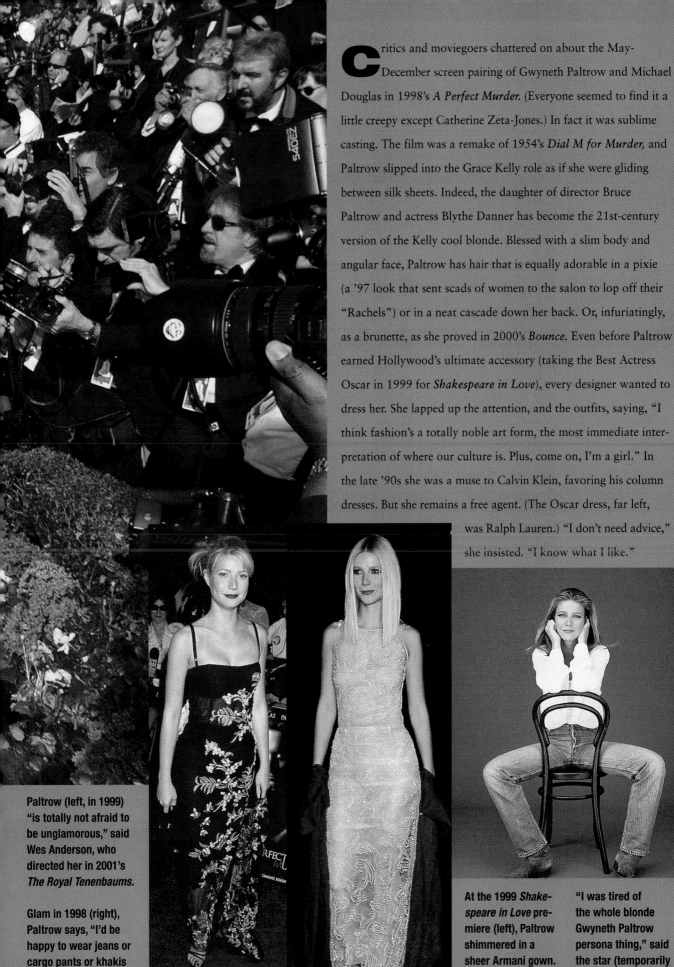

C ritics and moviegoers chattered on about the May-December screen pairing of Gwyneth Paltrow and Michael Douglas in 1998's *A Perfect Murder.* (Everyone seemed to find it a little creepy except Catherine Zeta-Jones.) In fact it was sublime casting. The film was a remake of 1954's *Dial M for Murder,* and Paltrow slipped into the Grace Kelly role as if she were gliding between silk sheets. Indeed, the daughter of director Bruce Paltrow and actress Blythe Danner has become the 21st-century version of the Kelly cool blonde. Blessed with a slim body and angular face, Paltrow has hair that is equally adorable in a pixie (a '97 look that sent scads of women to the salon to lop off their "Rachels") or in a neat cascade down her back. Or, infuriatingly, as a brunette, as she proved in 2000's *Bounce.* Even before Paltrow earned Hollywood's ultimate accessory (taking the Best Actress Oscar in 1999 for *Shakespeare in Love*), every designer wanted to dress her. She lapped up the attention, and the outfits, saying, "I think fashion's a totally noble art form, the most immediate interpretation of where our culture is. Plus, come on, I'm a girl." In the late '90s she was a muse to Calvin Klein, favoring his column dresses. But she remains a free agent. (The Oscar dress, far left, was Ralph Lauren.) "I don't need advice," she insisted. "I know what I like."

Paltrow (left, in 1999) "is totally not afraid to be unglamorous," said Wes Anderson, who directed her in 2001's *The Royal Tenenbaums.*

Glam in 1998 (right), Paltrow says, "I'd be happy to wear jeans or cargo pants or khakis every day."

At the 1999 *Shakespeare in Love* premiere (left), Paltrow shimmered in a sheer Armani gown.

"I was tired of the whole blonde Gwyneth Paltrow persona thing," said the star (temporarily brunette in 1993).

Tina Turner

In '60s minis or '80s pumps, the singer always had great legs. Her celebrated comeback proved her career did, too

She has sworn that the tiny skirts, a wardrobe staple since she sang with the Ikettes in the '60s, were more about camouflaging a short torso and not showing off those endless gams. "Nobody believes me, but I was never trying to project a sexy image," she said. "Even *I* look at the pictures sometimes and I think, 'Ha-ha, Tina, you weren't?'" At first her image was what Ike Turner made of the young Anna Mae Bullock. After she left him, and their abusive marriage, she restyled herself as an independent rock goddess. Her 1984 album *Private Dancer* sold 12 million copies and gave adolescent MTV viewers an eyeful of a fabulous 44-year-old in black heels and a mile of fishnet stockings. Sexy? "I just figured fishnets don't tear like regular hose."

"Tina is like a champion boxer. She has persistence, she has fortitude, she has pride" —*Sugar Ray Leonard*

In the '60s, Tina (on tour in 1981) "wore bone-straight white woman's wigs when black people were wearing Afros and saying, 'Say it loud, I'm black and I'm proud,'" recalled Ruth Carter, who costumed her 1993 film *What's Love Got to Do with It.*

If she had only the flashy looks but not the lightning speed, she still would have attracted attention. But for months surrounding the 1988 Olympics, Joyner was a headliner on the sports pages and in fashion coverage. At the trials, with one leg wrapped in spandex, the other bare as you please, she broke Evelyn Ashford's 100-meter record—four times in two days. In Seoul she wore the U.S. team uniform, but you could pick her out by her long, jewel-like nails (or just look for the woman with three gold and one silver medals swinging from her neck). The L.A. girl who once sewed custom clothes for her Barbie soon inspired a new generation. Among her rewards: a Flo-Jo doll, complete with a tiny one-legger and press-on nails.

"When I see her, the only thing that goes on in my mind is me in her shoes"
—a Flo-Jo fan and runner, age 16

FLORENCE GRIFFITH-JOYNER

With flair, polish—and some self-made tracksuits—the Olympics' most flamboyant flyer became the Queen of Seoul

81

BARBIE

She may be only 11½" tall, but she boasts a massive résumé and closet

"She can never bloat, rot, wrinkle or OD. And she has no children to betray her"
—*MG Lord, her unauthorized biographer*

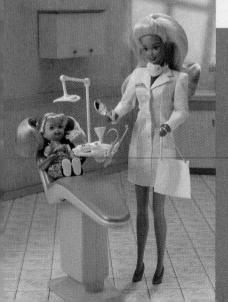

In 1997, Barbie added DDS to her impressive CV. She promised painless dentistry, except for the purchasing parents.

More than 1 billion Barbies (and pals) exist, making them the world's third largest population after China and India.

Born a teenager in 1959, Barbie had a maiden gig as a fashion model (left). Later, she toned down the makeup and arched brows.

More career- than family-oriented, Barbie (singing in 1995) never married Ken or had kids. Maybe even dolls can't have it all.

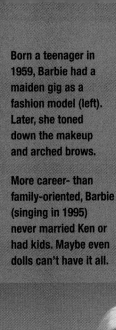

A bit of Barbie math: The average American girl owns eight Barbie dolls. Worldwide, two are sold every second. More staggering: She's over 40 now, and hasn't had a single nip, tuck or wrinkle lasering. If she could talk, she'd check out the mirror and say, "Damn, I look *good*!" Too good for some. Since her 1959 debut, parents and psychologists have worried about the effects of Barbie's improbable measurements (the equivalent of 36-18-33) on little girls' self-esteem and body image. Grown-ups, far more than kids, seem fixated on Barbie's figure and high-heel-ready pointed feet. But why not worry, instead, about Barbie influencing their daughters' future career plans? Can every girl grow up to be a supermodel–veterinarian–WNBA forward–astronaut–rock star–politician–CEO? According to her official bio, Barbie Millicent Roberts of Willows, Wis., did so with diplomas only from Willows High and an unnamed college. It's not that she can't commit to one profession, it's just that every job change means a whole new fabulous wardrobe. How can she choose? Fortunately, Barbie doesn't have to.

One small step for Barbie, one giant leap for plastic womanhood. She wasn't the first female in space, but the first in pink poofy sleeves.

The first black Barbie debuted in 1980. In 1999, designer Bob Mackie dressed this African princess.

Sporting the latest in teeny-tiny technology, executive Barbie took her cell phone and laptop computer to work in 1999.

TOP 10

TODAY'S HOT DESIGNERS
TO THE STARS

They are the creators who get the call before the opening of a film—or that all-important envelope

GIORGIO ARMANI

In 1991, *Women's Wear Daily* dubbed the Oscars "the Armani Awards," so dominant was the influential designer. Many in the U.S. first glimpsed the Milan-based Armani's work in 1980's *American Gigolo*, which showed off his unstructured suits, now a staple of Liam Neeson's wardrobe. But he also catered to women, like (with him, above) Sophia Loren.

> "A lot of people wear my clothes for their real lives, as well as when the flashbulbs are popping," said Armani. Fans include Jodie Foster (in '95) and Rosie Perez (in '99).

DONATELLA VERSACE

After her brother Gianni's 1997 murder, Versace became the head of his fashion house. (Brother Santo still crunches the numbers.) "There was no time to cry, only time to do the collection," she said after her first show. She has since hired 15 designers to back her up. Her perseverance after the tragedy has kept the family name—and its aesthetic of Louis XIV meets Marat Sade—popular with risqué dressers like Madonna and Christina Aguilera.

> In the male-dominated fashion industry, few designers slip into their own creations. But Versace wore Jennifer Lopez's 2000 Grammy dress first. Right: Faith Hill in 2000.

VALENTINO

After four decades in the trade, Italy's Valentino Garavani still gets excited to receive a call like the one placed by Courteney Cox—she needed a wedding gown. "This proves that a young girl, who can have dresses from everywhere, loves my things." From Jackie Onassis to Ashley Judd, women have swooned for his designs, usually in signature red, because, he said, "it's very sexy and powerful."

RANDOLPH DUKE

The son of a Las Vegas showgirl, Duke launched his own label in 1998, after two years at Halston. His following includes Jennifer Lopez and Hilary Swank, who wore a Duke creation to pick up her 2000 Best Actress Oscar. This year he dressed long-shot winner Marcia Gay Harden. Odds-makers in his home-town might check out who's in Duke in 2002.

Judd in 2000. Julia Roberts now owns the vintage (1980) classic she wore at the 2001 Oscars. Said a spokesperson for Valentino: "She can eat hamburgers in it if she likes."

"It was important to make her feel like a princess," said Duke of Swank, who wanted to just remind folks that the lead in *Boys Don't Cry* was a girl. Left: Minnie Driver in 2000.

JOHN GALLIANO

A Spaniard raised in London, he heads the French house of Dior to the delight of stars favoring his romanticism, like Tina Turner. His ideal client, he said, knows that "the lazy spiral of a bias-cut dress doesn't look like much on a hanger, but try it on and you discover the sex bomb that is waiting to be worn."

VERA WANG

A onetime *Vogue* editor, she made her first wedding gown for her own nuptials, then became the designer of choice among celebrity brides. Wang's trademark sheer "illusion" net fabric and streamlined designs turned up on evening wear for Holly Hunter and a skating outfit for Nancy Kerrigan at the '94 Olympics.

TOM FORD

"Gucci made its name dressing movie stars, because it had the dazzle they loved. I wanted to get that back," said Ford, a Texan who took over in 1994, when the legendary fashion house was best known for staid loafers. His up-to-date retro style drew back fans like Charlize Theron (above) and Gwyneth Paltrow.

"Fits like a glove," said Cate Blanchett in '99. If gloves were applied with a paintbrush

Columbia student Julia Stiles played hooky at the 2001 Oscars in this glittery Wang

"I'm proud to wear it," said Oscar presenter Helen Hunt of her Ford at the '99 awards

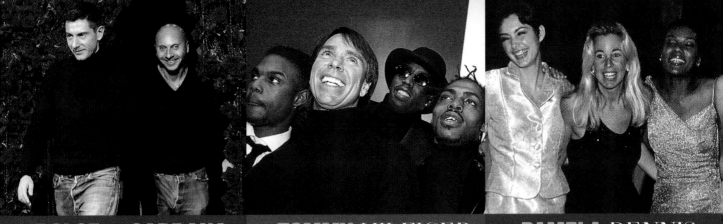

DOLCE & GABBANA

Italian partners Domenico Dolce and Stefano Gabbana share a simple philosophy. "When we design a dress," says Gabbana (left), "we try to imagine whether a man will whistle at the woman who wears it." Devotees include Whitney Houston, Mary J. Blige and, tellingly for a whole decade, the mercurial Madonna.

TOMMY HILFIGER

The Ralph Lauren protégé is a hit with Lenny Kravitz and Jewel, as well as hip-hoppers like (above, from left) Davante, Sean "Puffy" Combs and Coolio. Teens, too, get his across-the-dial appeal. "When you wear his clothes," said one in L.A., "you can relax. You know you're wearing something that's on TV, that's respected."

PAMELA DENNIS

Bette Midler and Calista Flock-hart know that Dennis (between models) offers glamour—plus a little mothering. (She made sure Liv Tyler's purse had tissues, in case the actress cried.) But not everyone needs input. "Lauren Holly once wore a dress of mine backwards," Dennis recalled. "It looked better, actually."

Angelina Jolie wore a D&G suit to stand out amid the wall-to-wall gowns at the 2001 Oscars.

Like many musicians, Jon Bon Jovi finds Hilfiger as comfortable onstage as off.

For the '99 Oscars, Tyler's preparation included this dress and a "serious bubble bath."

TOP 10

Who needed shoulder pads to camouflage a thick waist? Who was obsessed with her own navel? Only these legendary stylemakers know for sure

CLASSIC DESIGNERS TO THE STARS

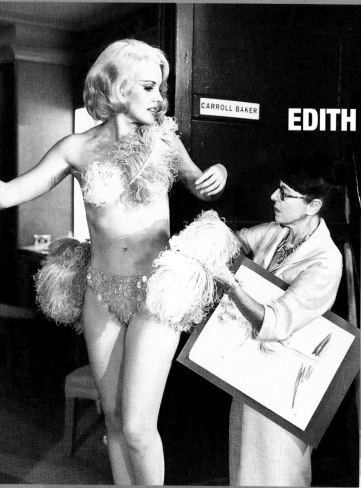

CARROLL BAKER

EDITH **HEAD**

"Other designers were busy starring their clothes in a film; Edith was making clothes to suit a character," raved Bette Davis, who wore Head's work in *All About Eve*. Head (with Carroll Baker) didn't care for avant fashion: "I'm a confirmed fence-sitter." She dedicated her life to dressing movies, lobbying the Academy to recognize wardrobe with an Oscar, and then winning seven. For 1982's *Dead Men Don't Wear Plaid*, Head recreated a dress she'd made in 1944 for Barbara Stanwyck in *Double Indemnity*—for Steve Martin. She zipped him into it, burst out laughing and said, "I've come full circle."

The chief designer for MGM in its golden age, Gilbert Adrian (born Adrian Adolph Greenberg) created Joan Crawford's severe shoulder pads in *The Women* (right, in 1939), Greta Garbo's finery in *Anna Christie* and Katharine Hepburn's wedding gown in *The Philadelphia Story*. Glamour came **ADRIAN** easily, but he also had a gift for injecting subtle styling into the clothes for downscale roles. He made Judy Garland's gingham dress for *The Wizard of Oz*, then carried the simple fabric into a couture line he developed after leaving the studio. American women, he proclaimed, "should be streamlined in the daytime, full of imagination at night."

Givenchy later admitted to an original disappointment: He thought it was his idol *Katharine* Hepburn who had requested him as a costumer for her next movie. But no, it was relative youngster Audrey Hepburn (then 22), who wanted him to outfit *Sabrina*. He told that story with great amusement, years after the designer and the star (left, in 1983) had become the best of friends and collaborators on five other films. Though he also dressed Elizabeth Taylor among others, he said, "No one was like Audrey. She really understood how she should look." Born to a noble French family, Givenchy began as an assistant to Cristobal Balenciaga and Elsa Schiaparelli. His notable clients included Rose Kennedy and Jacqueline Kennedy just before her husband's first trip to Paris. In 1995, the year that a *Sabrina* remake (with Julia Ormond) appeared, Givenchy retired, after more than 50 years in the business.

HUBERT DE GIVENCHY

The son of Russian nobility, Count Oleg Cassini was raised in Italy and educated in Paris before coming to the States and beginning his career as a studio costumer. In 1941, he eloped with actress Gene Tierney. Because they had no time for a wedding with a formal gown, he later designed one for her to wear onscreen in *The Razor's Edge*. After their divorce, Cassini dated Grace Kelly (right, with him in 1954), who broke his heart by leaving him for a prince. His luck changed professionally when Joe Kennedy recommended him to daughter-in-law Jacqueline, who made him the official couturier of the White House. Credited with her streamlined style, Cassini has said his goal was "to let her come through the dresses."

OLEG CASSINI

An assistant to Edith Head, Mackie emerged from her shadow on *The Carol Burnett Show*. He made the shimmery gowns in which the comedienne greeted her audience, as well as costumes for her sketches, memorably a Scarlett O'Hara "curtains" dress, complete with rod. Soon Diana Ross and Cher (right, in '88) lined up in Mackie's fitting room. The latter proved a kindred spirit in the love of skin and sequins. Drag actor Alexis Arquette is also a fan. "Mackie," he says, "is every cross-dresser's dream."

BOB MACKIE

At 21, the Algerian-born designer became the head of the house of Dior, a month after the death of Christian Dior. Nervous? "Not at all," he said, and the following year, 1958, he premiered his celebrated trapeze dress. But in 1959 he put alligator motorcycle jackets on the runway, got fired and was drafted into the army. Out by 1961, he started his own business with partner (and later lover) Pierre Bergé. His designs got a boost from Catherine Deneuve, who wore them as a high-end prostitute in *Belle de Jour* and three other films. Other fans include Shirley MacLaine (right, in 1965) and *Sex and the City*'s Kim Cattrall, who married in 1998 in a modern Saint Laurent slip dress.

YVES SAINT LAURENT

HALSTON

Born Roy Halston Frowick in Iowa, Halston launched himself as a milliner in Chicago, nabbing, as his first celeb client, Fran Allison, of *Kukla, Fran and Ollie*. Kim Novak and Carol Channing (left) then joined the list. In New York, his influence reached beyond mere stars: He designed Jackie Kennedy's inaugural pillbox. But when hats went out of favor, he made clothes—halter dresses and ultra-suede coats—becoming the dominant U.S. designer of the '70s. Dressing the elite, and partying with them at Studio 54, made his name. But Halston sold that valuable name to J.C. Penney, and died at 57, before the restoration of his house in the 1990s.

NINO **CERRUTI**

The Cerruti house dates back to 1881, when the northern Italian family began producing wool. In the 1950s, the founder's grandson Nino began turning luxury fabric into fine clothing and eventually into film wardrobes. His credits include Faye Dunaway in *Bonnie and Clyde*, Jack Nicholson's devil in *The Witches of Eastwick*, Richard Gere's millionaire in *Pretty Woman*, Harrison Ford's CIA hero in *Clear and Present Danger* and the 1994 couture movie *Ready to Wear* (whose premiere he attended, left, with actress Béatrice Dalle). Cerruti is still today the name Hollywood men want on their tuxedo label on Oscar night, and Nicholson accepted his award in one in 1998.

NOLAN MILLER

Thank Barbara Stanwyck, the matchmaker who introduced Miller to producer Aaron Spelling. For Spelling, Miller would design the flimsy crime-fighting outfits for *Charlie's Angels* as well as the gold-button armor of the warring vixens of *Dynasty* (above). "I was in heaven," he said. "This show was all about the lifestyle of the ultimately wealthy. I could be as extravagant as I wanted." He could also improvise, coming to Heather Locklear's rescue with a last-minute wedding gown for her 1994 marriage to Richie Sambora. For those who, like Miller, are terminally *Dynasty*-obsessed, his costume jewels are available on the shopping channel QVC.

Born Ralph Lifshitz and raised with three siblings in a two-bedroom Bronx apartment, he dreamed of a lush life out of reach for his blue-collar family. A devotee of F. Scott Fitzgerald, he toiled as a stockboy in order to buy Brooks Brothers jackets. When he achieved early success in 1969 with neckties, he named his company after a sport never played in his old neighborhood but evoking the old-money image he was after. "I believe in clothes that are not dated," said the founder of Polo, and he was the perfect choice to interpret the '20s in the '70s for *The Great Gatsby* (starring Robert Redford, above). Three decades on, he is still a favorite of the likes of Gwyneth Paltrow, who collected her 1999 Oscar in a pink Lauren creation.

RALPH LAUREN

TWIGGY

Initially rejected by magazines as too skinny, Twiggy (Lesley Hornby) cracked the London fashion scene after a haircut that took seven hours to perfect. Capped by the new look (left), she was hailed as the Face of 1966. The next year, met by a flurry of press at New York's JFK airport, she was asked about her figure and replied, "Not really what you'd call a figure, is it?" Girls dieted feverishly to get Twiggy thin, but the model herself was able to eat "everything—chocolate, potatoes—because I was desperate to put on weight."

Sticklike or curvy, tall or . . . *really* tall, these star clothes hangers strode from magazines and runways into lasting fashion fame

TOP 10
ALL-TIME
MODELS

CHERYL TIEGS

The epitome of the sunny California image, she actually hailed from Minnesota. The 1960s teen model gained her greatest fame in 1970, in her first of 10 SPORTS ILLUSTRATED swimsuit editions. (Above, the 1983 cover.) With a record-breaking Cover Girl cosmetics contract, and her image on the cover of TIME, Tiegs was among the first mannequins known by name, not just by pretty face.

NAOMI CAMPBELL

"No money or prestige could further justify the abuse that has been imposed [by Campbell]," said her modeling agency, explaining why it had dropped one of the world's most statuesque and remunerated models. Eventually, the London-based Campbell (in 1998) cooled down, and renewed her contract. At that point she reportedly took an anger management course to quell the beast behind the beauty.

KATE MOSS

"FEED ME," implored graffiti scrawled across Moss's naked torso. The English model with the preadolescent build stirred public concern: Was she eating enough? Would their daughters waste away to imitate her "waif" look? "Hello? I do eat," said Moss (in 1995), responding to the worry of the world. The pendulum then swung back to curvy girls, but Moss's career has outlasted the brief, scary trend she launched.

BROOKE SHIELDS

What came between Shields and her Calvins? "Nothing," she cooed in provocative ads. But to temper that image, the 6' model became a spokeswoman for abstinence, too. Once the Ivory Snow baby, Shields (in the '80s) grew equally famous for unfashionably thick eyebrows. "Spending any unnecessary time grooming myself just didn't appeal," said the Princeton alum.

93

The story goes that at an early shoot for a fabric company, the designer didn't have enough material to cover even tiny Jean Shrimpton. No matter, just make the dress smaller, she instructed. Voilà. Minis now ruled, and Shrimpton (in 1960), a graduate from a posh London modeling school, became the queen of the short skirt. Along with photographer and then-boyfriend David Bailey, she was part of a '60s scene that TIME dubbed "swinging London." Retired from modeling, she now runs an English inn.

JEAN SHRIMPTON

CLAUDIA SCHIFFER

A talent scout found the 17-year-old German student dancing at a Dusseldorf disco. Schiffer didn't believe him when he said she could be a model. Though he spoke to her parents about working in Paris, and got her several shoots there, she later said she believed his pitch only after her face first appeared on the cover of *Elle*. Soon she was a favorite of Guess? jeans, Chanel and Revlon. The 1990s answer to Brigitte Bardot, Schiffer (in 1995) recently lent her style savvy to a Palm Pilot edition, customized with her favorite software.

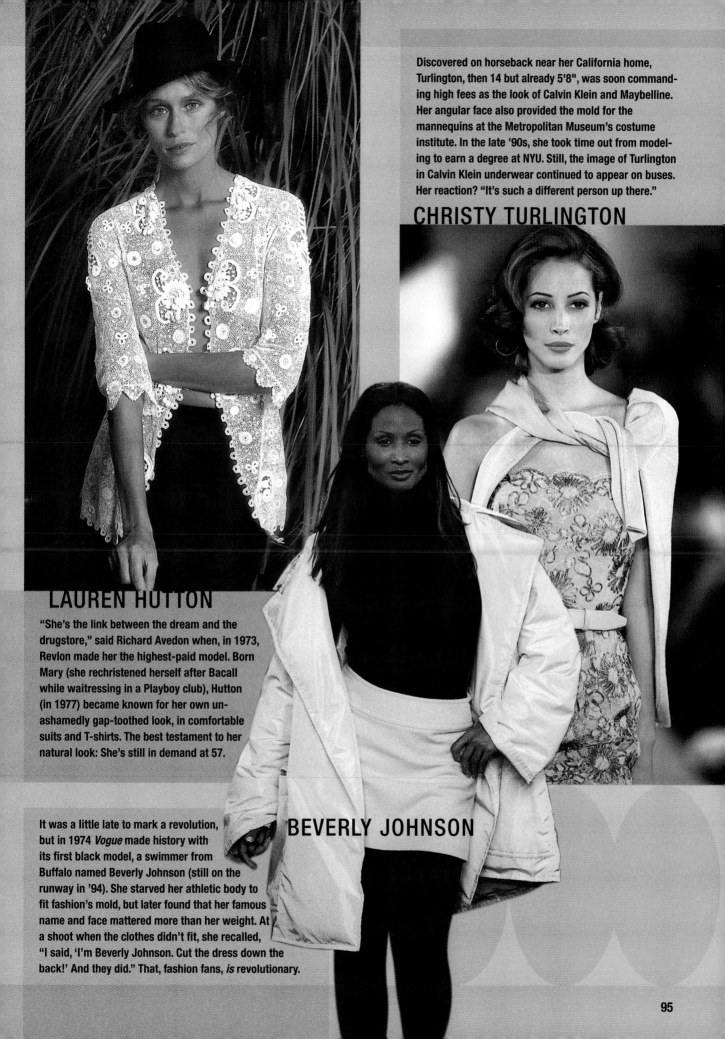

Discovered on horseback near her California home, Turlington, then 14 but already 5'8", was soon commanding high fees as the look of Calvin Klein and Maybelline. Her angular face also provided the mold for the mannequins at the Metropolitan Museum's costume institute. In the late '90s, she took time out from modeling to earn a degree at NYU. Still, the image of Turlington in Calvin Klein underwear continued to appear on buses. Her reaction? "It's such a different person up there."

CHRISTY TURLINGTON

LAUREN HUTTON

"She's the link between the dream and the drugstore," said Richard Avedon when, in 1973, Revlon made her the highest-paid model. Born Mary (she rechristened herself after Bacall while waitressing in a Playboy club), Hutton (in 1977) became known for her own unashamedly gap-toothed look, in comfortable suits and T-shirts. The best testament to her natural look: She's still in demand at 57.

BEVERLY JOHNSON

It was a little late to mark a revolution, but in 1974 *Vogue* made history with its first black model, a swimmer from Buffalo named Beverly Johnson (still on the runway in '94). She starved her athletic body to fit fashion's mold, but later found that her famous name and face mattered more than her weight. At a shoot when the clothes didn't fit, she recalled, "I said, 'I'm Beverly Johnson. Cut the dress down the back!' And they did." That, fashion fans, *is* revolutionary.

Girl POWER!

Pow! Bam! Thank you, ma'am! Not since the Age of the Amazons have women wielded such fabulous force

Perils? Pauline needed aid in 1947. Today's gals have consigned helplessness to history.

Diana Rigg
AS EMMA PEEL

A dominatrix counterpoint to button-down Mr. Steed, the cat-suited crime fighter made a cult hit of *The Avengers.* In 1999, *TV Guide* heralded the British actress, now Dame Diana, as the tube's "most completely liberated woman."

Brigitte Nielsen
AS THE GREAT DANE

At the end of her on- and offscreen pairing with Sylvester Stallone (*Rocky IV, Cobra* and 19 months of wedlock), the 6' actress became a model survivor, rebuilding a life as a Copenhagen talk show host.

Sarah Michelle Gellar
AS BUFFY THE VAMPIRE SLAYER

"I wish growing up that there were characters like that that I could watch," said Gellar of her prime-time alter ego. "Buffy is an incredible role model: She's not the most popular, she's not the smartest in school, and she's an individual. The hardest thing to learn as a teenager is individuality." Nothing like battling the undead between midterms to set you apart from the crowd.

97

Angelina Jolie
AS LARA CROFT

When the video game Tomb Raider debuted in 1996, its pneumatic star was aimed at adolescent boys. But girls grabbed the joysticks, happy to see a female protagonist. An archaeologist more like Indiana Jones than Mary Leakey, Croft was fleshed out in 2001 by Jolie. She'd never played the game but, upon checking it out, recalled thinking, "Oh boy, there's a woman who makes me look average and feel inferior."

Lindsay Wagner
AS THE BIONIC WOMAN

As with Dr. Frankenstein, the creators of *The Six Million Dollar Man* saw that their creature needed a mate. She in turn would need her own TV series (and a bionic German shepherd, Max). In 1974 Wagner became Jaime Sommers, a tennis pro who after an accident is revived with mechanical parts that give her the gifts of superspeed and long-range hearing. Though seemingly made for her man, the pair didn't wed until a reunion movie, two decades later.

No shrinking violets, action heroines put petal to the metal, playing virtuous avengers to the hilt

Zhang Zi Yi and Michelle Yeoh
IN *Crouching Tiger, Hidden Dragon*

In most martial arts films, women are plot points to spur Bruce Lee or Jackie Chan into action. But in 2000's foreign film Oscar winner, veteran Yeoh (right; she had previously taken on Chan and James Bond) and newcomer Zhang flew over rooftops, wielding swords and fists. Also in the cast was Cheng Pei Pei, who began chopping onscreen in 1965 and observed, "You needed to show not only the soft and pretty side, but also an energy. If you only act tough, then it's like you are a man."

Lucy Lawless
AS *Xena: Warrior Princess*

A recurring character on the 1990s *Hercules* series, Xena was an evil renegade Amazon. As a headliner, she softened a bit, becoming a fighter for justice; 5'10" New Zealand actress Lawless starred and did her own stunt work. Producers foresaw problems when Lawless planned to have a baby. Not to worry: Costumers were permitted use of anachronistic spandex, and writers made her TV's first pregnant superhero.

Irish McCalla
AS *Sheena, Queen of the Jungle*

The mark of a classic is that future generations return to the well. So it is with Sheena, a 1930s comic about a girl raised by a witch doctor after her explorer dad dies, who grows up to unravel terrorist plots while wearing a leopard bikini. In the 1950s, McCalla filled the skins. In 2000, it was *Baywatch* alum Gena Lee Nolin, who reinterprets the character as a scantily clad environmentalist.

99

Faye Dunaway
IN *BONNIE AND CLYDE*

The life of a Depression-era blonde bank robber who could handle a tommy gun as well as the boys has hit the big screen at least five times, including a 1958 film noir treatment with Dorothy Provine. But Bonnie Parker's legend is tied to Dunaway (as that of her husband, Clyde Barrow, is to Warren Beatty, left, in '67). Parker, said Dunaway, "is the closest thing to me: a frustrated Southern girl who wanted to break out."

Mae West
AS THE *PROVOCATEUR*

West emerged from the burlesque circuit to create her sexually uninhibited persona in plays and movie scripts that gave her lines like "It's not the men in your life, it's the life in your men." Her first stage show, called *Sex,* landed her in jail on obscenity charges. But Hollywood embraced her brassy, buxom turns in *I'm No Angel* and *My Little Chickadee* (left, 1940). Censors eventually pushed her out of the biz, but she returned at 78 in *Myra Breckridge.*

> Never mind the ring finger—the dynamic digit is the one that squeezes the trigger, stopping a man dead in his tracks

Sigourney Weaver
IN *ALIEN*

Just before the casting of the 1979 original, space survivalist Ripley got a tantalizing sex change. "No one would ever think the girl is going to end up the hero," said Weaver. And, in three sequels (left, the first, in 1986), she outlasted the extraterrestrial bug—and most of the humans. Every time the alien picked someone off, the actress sent her late costar condolence flowers.

Barbara Stanwyck
AS ANNIE OAKLEY

At 8, Phoebe Anne Moses learned to hunt to feed her family after her father died in 1865. Using a stage name, she later became the shooting star of Buffalo Bill's road show. Just nine years after Oakley's death, Stanwyck (only hinting at future hardboiled portrayals) starred in a 1935 biopic. In the '40s, Ethel Merman recaptured her frontier feminism in a Broadway musical; Betty Hutton headlined the Hollywood version of *Annie Get Your Gun*.

Linda Hamilton
IN *TERMINATOR 2*

Re-creating her role as Sarah Connor, Hamilton had an image in mind of what her warrior-mama should look like: "My goal [was] to have Madonna's body." Her newly buffed biceps made toting Uzis a breeze. When the sequel came out in 1991, it sent women racing to health clubs. "Most don't say, 'I want to build strength,'" reported one trainer. "They say, 'I want to look like Linda Hamilton.'"

Jane Fonda
AS BARBARELLA

Director (and Fonda's then husband) Roger Vadim intended his swinging 1968 space sex odyssey to be sophisticated. In fact, it appeared to have been shot on the cheese side of the moon: In the year 4000, the cartoonish heroine saves the universe after surviving an attack from wind-up cannibal dolls and from birds eating away her barely there costume. Only a woman of real force could live down this role, as Fonda admirably did.

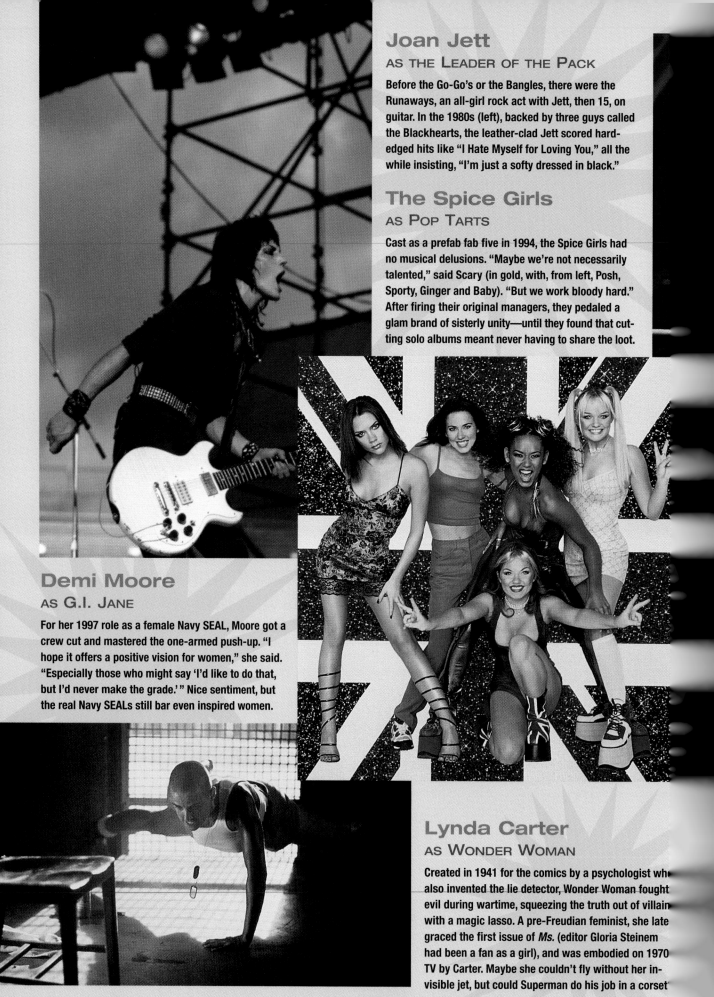

Joan Jett
AS THE LEADER OF THE PACK

Before the Go-Go's or the Bangles, there were the Runaways, an all-girl rock act with Jett, then 15, on guitar. In the 1980s (left), backed by three guys called the Blackhearts, the leather-clad Jett scored hard-edged hits like "I Hate Myself for Loving You," all the while insisting, "I'm just a softy dressed in black."

The Spice Girls
AS POP TARTS

Cast as a prefab fab five in 1994, the Spice Girls had no musical delusions. "Maybe we're not necessarily talented," said Scary (in gold, with, from left, Posh, Sporty, Ginger and Baby). "But we work bloody hard." After firing their original managers, they pedaled a glam brand of sisterly unity—until they found that cutting solo albums meant never having to share the loot.

Demi Moore
AS G.I. JANE

For her 1997 role as a female Navy SEAL, Moore got a crew cut and mastered the one-armed push-up. "I hope it offers a positive vision for women," she said. "Especially those who might say 'I'd like to do that, but I'd never make the grade.'" Nice sentiment, but the real Navy SEALs still bar even inspired women.

Lynda Carter
AS WONDER WOMAN

Created in 1941 for the comics by a psychologist who also invented the lie detector, Wonder Woman fought evil during wartime, squeezing the truth out of villains with a magic lasso. A pre-Freudian feminist, she later graced the first issue of *Ms.* (editor Gloria Steinem had been a fan as a girl), and was embodied on 1970 TV by Carter. Maybe she couldn't fly without her invisible jet, but could Superman do his job in a corset

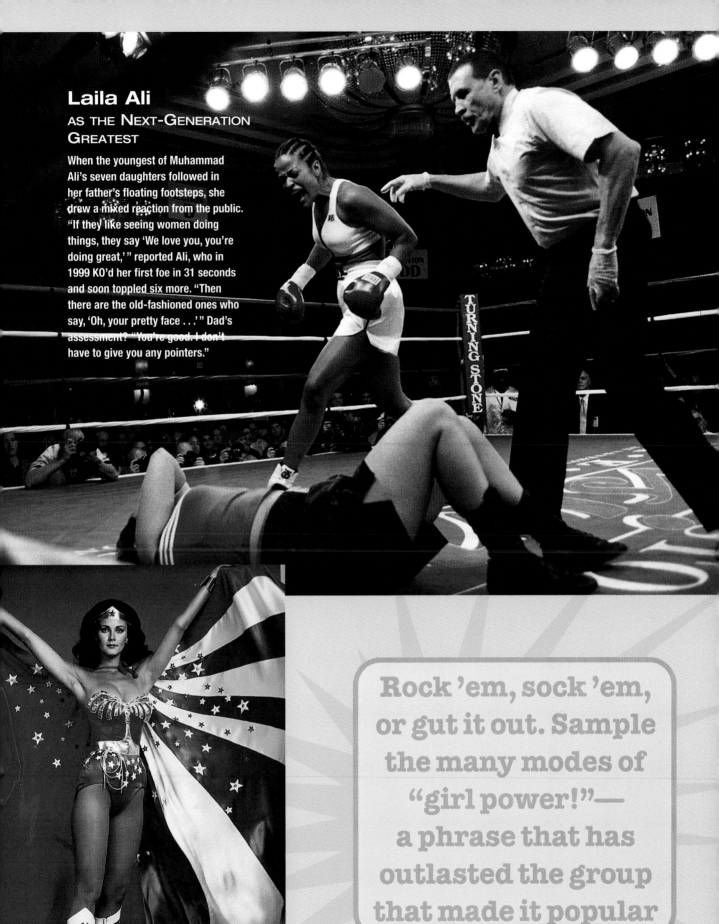

Laila Ali

AS THE NEXT-GENERATION GREATEST

When the youngest of Muhammad Ali's seven daughters followed in her father's floating footsteps, she drew a mixed reaction from the public. "If they like seeing women doing things, they say 'We love you, you're doing great,'" reported Ali, who in 1999 KO'd her first foe in 31 seconds and soon toppled six more. "Then there are the old-fashioned ones who say, 'Oh, your pretty face . . .'" Dad's assessment? "You're good. I don't have to give you any pointers."

Rock 'em, sock 'em, or gut it out. Sample the many modes of "girl power!"— a phrase that has outlasted the group that made it popular

Jenna Elfman
LIGHT FANTASTIC

She made her way by following in Goldie Hawn's flower-strewn hippy-dippy path, but Elfman put a smart, yogic '90s twist on the daffy sprite. Playing for laughs on *Dharma & Greg* isn't a stretch for Elfman, who has said, "There's a lot of myself in the character—her freeness, her playfulness. I feel that it comes off the screen how much fun I'm having."

Brigitte Bardot
THE BUTTERY BAGUETTE

God created woman, but director Roger Vadim made his auburn-haired girlfriend a blonde. Her artful dishevelment in Vadim's 1956 *And God Created Woman* catapulted her to fame. But Bardot (in *La Parisienne,* 1957) never embraced her sex-kitten image, and at 40 she retired to crusade for animal rights.

A Brief History of Blonde

Good goddess! Flouting propriety and flaunting their stuff, blondes have ranged from dangerous to ditzy, flinty to fabulous, virtuous to va-va-voom. Dumb? Not judging by their box office clout

Jean Harlow
THE PLATINUM STANDARD

Her agent dubbed her the Platinum Blonde and, with a promotional stunt for the 1931 film of the same name, raised peroxide sales 35 percent as women tried to match Harlow's hue. Eventually her own stylist revealed his recipe, which included ammonia, Clorox and Lux flakes. After repeated applications, however, it caused the young star's hair to become brittle and fall out.

Whether playing it cool and unattainable or slinging hash in a diner, the elegant blonde is always luminous

Veronica Lake
PEEKING BOB

Her eye-obscuring hairdo came about when Lake (then billed as Constance Keane) let a few locks come untucked from behind her ear during a scene in 1940's *Forty Little Mothers*. The director, Busby Berkeley, loved it. (But her costar Eddie Cantor complained that it made her look like a sheepdog.) So popular was the peekaboo style that during World War II, Lake had to instruct women working in factories to tuck their hair back so it wouldn't get caught in the machinery.

Michelle Pfeiffer
TEQUILA SUNRISE

Having come up long after Holly-wood's glamour heyday, Pfeiffer is a throwback. Her effortless glow (rooted in a Southern California upbringing and beauty-pageant past) demands that modern audiences suspend dis-belief. Witness Pfeiffer in films like *Frankie and Johnny*—a coffee shop waitress who looks like *that*? Or *Dangerous Minds*—who ever had a high school teacher like *her*?

Catherine Deneuve
BELLE TOUJOURS

Decades after her breakthrough in 1967's *Belle du Jour*, Deneuve recalled why director Luis Buñuel had cast her as the upper-class wife turned call girl: "He wanted a blonde, cold-looking woman . . . not too sensuous or too sexual." Hmm. Looking much as she did then, France's exquisite beauty continues to fog the lens on both sides of the Atlantic.

Lauren Bacall
MATCHLESS

At 19 she stole Bogie's heart, and seduced movie-goers by leaning in a hotel room doorway and growling, "Anybody got a match?" The scene—and a subsequent onscreen whistling lesson—made the steely ash-blonde (born Betty Joan Persky, in New York City) a star in 1944's *To Have and Have Not.* Said one critic about the source of Bacall's appeal: "She must have a panther in her family tree."

Drew Barrymore
THE THROWBACK

Baby fair in *E.T.*, the still-sweet film scion played up her neo-flower-child image and created a 1990s craze by tucking daisies into her curls. Though Barrymore went red in *Charlie's Angels* (produced by her own Flower Films Co.), her favorite hue was Marilyn-bright in *Batman Forever:* "It made me look like a really, really great dish."

Renée Zellweger
THE CHAMELEON

"She reminds you of a sister, a friend, someone you were in love with once," said *Jerry Maguire* director Cameron Crowe of Zellweger. But the Texas girl-next-door has stretched to play a New York Orthodox Jew and English diarist Bridget Jones.

Judy Holliday
THE SMART COOKIE

Born Judith Tuvim, she adopted the dummy act along with her stage name. "Like all great clowns, Judy could also move you," said George Cukor, who directed her to an Oscar in 1950's *Born Yesterday.* "She was a supreme technician. She made you laugh, and suddenly you were touched."

Goldie Hawn
PRECIOUS METTLE

Who ever thought that a girl who couldn't tell a joke on the '60s hit *Laugh-In* without collapsing in giggles would last long enough to deliver the line "The three stages of an actress's career are babe, district attorney and *Driving Miss Daisy*."

The Brady Girls
SISTER ACT

Marcia was inarguably the grooviest. Cindy was the baby with the adorable curls. And Jan—well, Jan had really long hair. Siblings had not battled so for attention since *King Lear*. Playing the female half of the '70s *Brady Bunch* kids gave (from left) Eve Plumb, Susan Olsen and Maureen McCormick their careers. Unfortunately, the indelibly sunny Brady image effectively outshined any future roles.

Lisa Kudrow
FROSTED FLAKE

A biology major at Vassar, Kudrow thought she'd try acting before med school. But this smart girl had a knack for playing airheads, first as the spaced-out waitress Ursula on *Mad About You,* then as Ursula's twin Phoebe on *Friends*. "Life's a lot easier when you're dumb," she said of the roles. "You don't take things personally because you're too dumb to get it."

Robert Redford
THE NATURAL

Breaking the "tall, dark and handsome" mold, Redford (in the mid-1970s) recast the Hollywood dreamboat in his own sun-dappled image. Mellowing with age, Redford the director cast leads after his own likeness: Brad Pitt and Matt Damon both took turns before Redford's lens.

Meg Ryan
SWEETNESS AND LIGHT?

This former homecoming queen rejects her America's Sweetheart label, maintaining that she's more complex than cute. (But wasn't it just sheer wholesomeness that let her get away with that famous fake orgasm in 1989's *When Harry Met Sally*?) Her much-imitated cropped cut? Not fashion, Ryan insists, but a practical choice for a working mom.

Cameron Diaz
THE REAL THING

"A genuine sex bomb with the gift of comic timing," raved a critic of Diaz's debut in *The Mask*. She then stole the high-grossing 1998 gross-out flick *There's Something About Mary* (right). But the star plays down the untouchable-blonde angle. "I wanted [my] characters to be accessible," she said. "I didn't want girls to go to the movie and say, 'Oh my god, I can never be like that.'"

Brad Pitt
THE SURE THING

"Wouldn't it be great if I was in a movie and some people didn't even recognize it was me?" Pitt (in 1998) once mused. That kind of talk no doubt shakes film producers to the core of their wallets. "I guess," he clarified, "I want people to say something more about me than 'He's cute.'"

James King
BLONDE ON THE BRINK

She did the model thing: Discovered in Omaha, moved to New York at 15, had too much fun and checked into rehab at 18. Now 22 and back in control of her charmed life, she's ready to do the acting thing. Her first year out, King's Midwestern beauty will grace no fewer than four films. Next comes the fame thing.

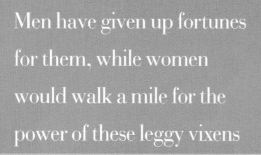

Men have given up fortunes for them, while women would walk a mile for the power of these leggy vixens

Daryl Hannah
WELL GROUNDED

When there's a role of a doctor or lawyer, people just go, "No, too blonde," moaned Hannah, whom casting folk more easily envisioned as a fish in *Splash* than a human professional. "Just because I've played ethereal doesn't mean I am ethereal. I'm certainly not a mermaid, you know."

Ivana Trump
THE EQUALIZER

"Don't get mad, get even," trilled the über First Wife. When her husband, the real estate tycoon Donald Trump, took up with a younger blonde, she packed her bags and phoned her lawyer. But not in that order. The former Czech ski bunny now sells her own brand of beauty on the Home Shopping channel.

Heather Locklear
LOVE-HATE RELATIONSHIP

Yes, she was a cop on *T.J. Hooker*, and a campaign aide on *Spin City*. But *Dynasty* and *Melrose Place* cemented Locklear's status as the schemer we love to hate. Said producer Aaron Spelling: "The fan mail we had to answer almost broke us."

Cybill Shepherd
SHE'S STILL GOT IT

"One of my mottos," Shepherd revealed not long ago, "is flaunt what you've got left." The model became an actress for 1971's *The Last Picture Show*. Now 51, she still turns up at cabaret appearances in asset-revealing gowns. Not because she clings to ingenue status. But because she can.

Morgan Fairchild
RHYMES WITH RICH

"In Hollywood, it's always 'We need a bitch—let's get Morgan,'" she once lamented. Strange predicament for the former Patsy McClenny, whom kids called Fatsy Patsy. Back then she aspired to be a scientist: "Pasteur, Jenner and Lister were my heroes." Instead she used alchemy to transform herself.

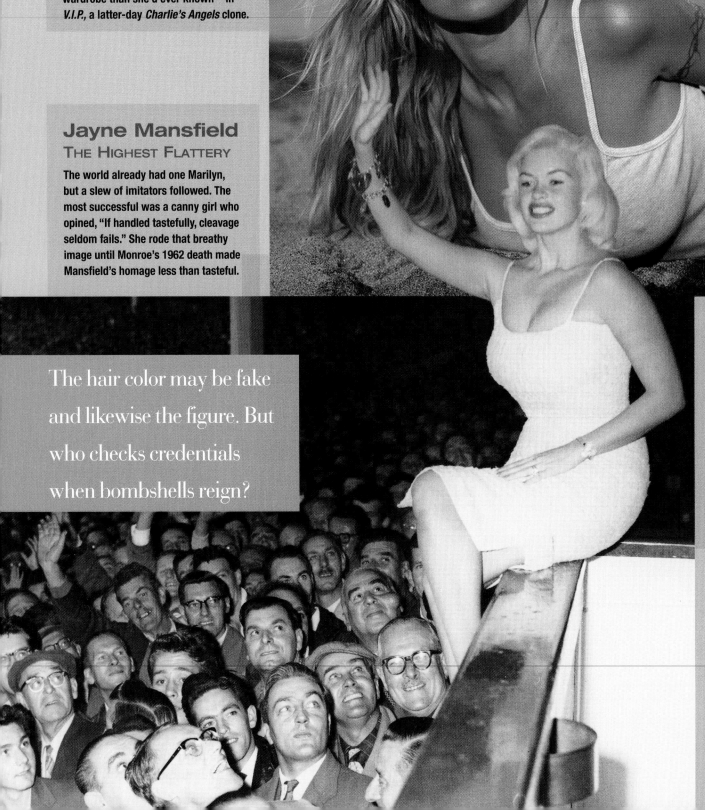

Pamela Anderson
DA BOMB

A pinup for the Internet age, Anderson is a self-made sex goddess who sends up her silicone image even as she lives it. The former *Baywatch*er got her big-screen beachhead playing, appropriately, a comic-book character come to life in 1996's *Barb Wire,* but then returned to TV—and more wardrobe than she'd ever known—in *V.I.P.,* a latter-day *Charlie's Angels* clone.

Jayne Mansfield
THE HIGHEST FLATTERY

The world already had one Marilyn, but a slew of imitators followed. The most successful was a canny girl who opined, "If handled tastefully, cleavage seldom fails." She rode that breathy image until Monroe's 1962 death made Mansfield's homage less than tasteful.

The hair color may be fake and likewise the figure. But who checks credentials when bombshells reign?

Courtney Love
CELEBRITY SKIN

When Love put down her guitar to star in 1996's *The People vs. Larry Flynt,* she also left behind her baby-doll dresses and smeared makeup. Soon she appeared on the red carpet transformed, though still with her rock-girl attitude. "It's the contradiction that makes her stand out," said designer Michael Kors.

Debbie Harry
THE BLONDE LEADING BLONDIE

The former Playboy bunny and hairdresser knew that the punk boys club needed some sex and femininity. So, backed by four men, Harry fronted Blondie, fusing rock, disco, rap, calypso—whatever struck her fancy. Nearly two decades after the band's breakup, Harry remains a hip New York icon: "The average person has to look for something to do on a Saturday night. Whereas me, I *am* Saturday night."

Christina Aguilera
BOTTLE BLONDE

Swiveling sexily in the video for her breakout 1999 hit "Genie in a Bottle" cued fans that Aguilera wasn't a Mousketeer anymore. For those over 13, you can tell her apart from her fellow Mickey Mouse Club alumna Britney Spears, because Aguilera's locks are whiter than Brit's, and because she sometimes sings in Spanish, a nod to her father's Latin roots.

RED Zone

Gents supposedly prefer blondes, but not a few hold a torch for reds ranging from apple-pie sweet to chili-pepper hot

Reba McEntire
GINGER SNAP

Known for hair as big as Texas and red as Georgia clay, the singer worried about trimming her tresses to a neat bob in 1996. McEntire capitalized on the predictable uproar in the country music world by sending out a lock of her hair (actually a snip from a well-matched wig) with each promotional CD.

Shirley MacLaine
RED ROVER

With 51 films and 7 books to her credit, it's understandable when MacLaine asserts, "I never had the patience for glamour. Hair—wash and dry, that's it. I've got better things to do." But long before the kid from Virginia became a star and world-renowned past-lives guru, she had revealed that "Rita Hayworth was my role model."

Ann-Margret
ORANGE CRUSH

From the moment her candy-colored mane emerged from a turtleneck sweater in *Bye Bye Birdie*, the Swedish-born star had America entranced with her tabby-cat charm. But breaking the kittenish mold, she leapt from *Birdie* and *Viva Las Vegas* to Oscar-nominated performances in *Carnal Knowledge* and *Tommy*.

Wynonna Judd
COUNTRY CRIMSON

The singer is up-front about being an out-of-the-box red: At a charity garage sale she offered up a package of her Tiger Lily dye. And while touring with her bandmate, mother Naomi, she said, "Our ambition is to change our hair color every week." Added Mom: "To something not found in nature."

Lucille Ball
TOP TOMATO

Love Lucy without her scarlet hair? Desi Arnaz did—his future wife was a blonde when they met. But MGM didn't and made their contract player over with a tint so unbelievable, critics commented that no one had hair that color. Ball's response: "I do." The star maintained its upkeep with an in-home hair salon.

Jessica Rabbit
PAINTED LADY

"I'm not bad; I'm just drawn that way," cooed the co-star of *Who Framed Roger Rabbit?* in the voice of the very blonde Kathleen Turner.

Rita Hayworth
FLAMETHROWER

In the midst of their divorce, Orson Welles was directing Hayworth in 1948's *The Lady from Shanghai*. Under the guise of auteurism, Welles ordered the star's locks bleached blonde and cut. Fans were appalled. During the war, Hayworth's red had been as patriotic as red, white and blue: Her pinup poster cheered GIs, and her image adorned the first nuke, earning her bragging rights as a nonblonde bombshell.

Angie Everhart
CINNAMON STICK

The 5'10" model from Akron, Ohio, leapt from the pages of SPORTS ILLUSTRATED's swimsuit edition into such film epics as *Bordello of Blood*. One of the few auburn beauties to come by her color naturally (her mom's a redhead too), Everhart has described her hue as "a shiny copper penny in the light with an old copper penny mixed in."

Sarah Ferguson
ROYAL FLUSH

Prince Andrew once called his bride's strawberry blonde hair her crowning glory. But follicle lust is a thin basis for a marriage, and theirs ended after 10 years, leaving Fergie as one of the world's top-paid redheaded pitchwomen.

Julianne Moore
BLOOD SIMPLE

"It's as bad as having to wear a purple shirt all the time," complained Moore when asked about her naturally cinnamon hair. "As an actor, the last thing you want is to be identified." Still, she shouldn't knock her red roots as they set up her stage debut: In a junior high *You're a Good Man, Charlie Brown*, she notes, "I had a nonspeaking role as the little red-haired girl."

Molly Ringwald
CHERRY ON TOP

"Ain't She Sweet?" asked a TIME cover about Ringwald in the 1980s, when she ruled teen cinema. Then the queen of screen angst kissed off Hollywood for Paris. In the late '90s she returned and, it seems, not a moment too soon. Who else to address issues like can a redhead wear red? "They say you can't," she told a curious paper. "But you can, and I do."

Maureen O'Hara
IRISH ROSE

In the early days of color film, some directors stuck with familiar black-and-white stock. Technicians using the new medium cheered whenever ginger-haired, emerald-eyed O'Hara was cast on a project, for they knew they'd be working too. They soon anointed her the Queen of Technicolor.

Red Skelton
CARROT SHTICK

The son of a circus clown, the former Richard Skelton re-created his vaudeville act in flicks like *Seeing Red* and *The Broadway Buckaroo*. Later, he honed his slapstick skills as a protégé of Buster Keaton. But it was his 20-some years on television (some of them in living color) that brought the widest audience for indelible characters like Clem Kadiddle-hopper or Cauliflower McPugg.

Danny Bonaduce
FIRECRACKER

The freckle-faced kid with grown-up comic timing stood out and stole the show from his blander *Partridge Family* screen siblings. Unfortunately, his precociousness didn't translate into adult success. After embarrassing arrests for drug possession and punching a transvestite prostitute, he settled in behind the mike of a Los Angeles radio station.

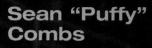

Sean "Puffy" Combs

HEAVEN'S HUE

"I feel safe in white because, deep down inside, I'm an angel," said hip-hop mogul Combs, known as much for this look as for the star-packed Labor Day parties at his Hamptons beach house, to which every guest was required to wear white. Why the dress code? "It kills the intention of outshining anyone else."

Men in White

Don't underestimate the understated elegance of ivory on a comic, a singer, a literary light—or even a poultry pitchman

Tom Wolfe
THE WHITE STUFF

The *Bonfire of the Vanities* author dropped his signature tint during Travolta's disco reign. "I bought a yellow suit [that] turned out to be really loud," he said. "If I wear it in public, dogs bark and small children leave the street crying."

John Travolta
STAYING POWER

At a 1979 charity auction, film critic Gene Siskel ventured $2,000 for the polyester duds that made Travolta a star in *Saturday Night Fever.* After the actor's 1994 comeback in *Pulp Fiction,* Siskel sold the suit for $146,000.

Steve Martin
DOES THIS LOOK FUNNY?

What does the fashionable man (ca. 1978) wear with a balloon-animal hat or an arrow through his head? For Martin—who dropped the monochromatic getup once he began making movies—the suit was a practical choice. "I knew my physical stuff was important," the comic once explained. "White would just make it stand out."

Mark Twain
JUST THE FLAX

Accounts of his wardrobe have been greatly exaggerated: Famous as early as the 1860s, Twain didn't don his iconic linen suit until a congressional appearance in 1906.

Smokey Robinson and the Miracles
COLOR-BLIND

Motown's premier vocal group performed with matching tunics and equally complementary harmonies. Songwriter Robinson (second from right) penned hits like "The Tears of a Clown" and "I Second That Emotion" with the goal, he once said, "not to make black music, just good music."

Fantasy Island
STRONG SUIT

"Fresh and clean" is how Ricardo Montalban described the uniform worn by his Mr. Roarke and Herve Villechaize's Tattoo. But after a day in costume, "I come home and put on a black robe."

Cab Calloway
COTTON CLUBBER

Marrying the 1930s zoot suit with white tie and tails, Harlem bandleader Calloway was, in his words, "togged to the bricks." The singer famous for scatting his way through "Minnie the Moocher" defined that phrase and others in his 1944 *Hepster's Dictionary*.

Don Johnson
THE BLAZER'S EDGE

Traditionalists thought Johnson (and *Miami Vice* partner Philip Michael Thomas) needed a shave and a tailor. Why the rolled sleeves? Can no one make a hem in South Florida? Paired with sherbet-colored shirts, their leisure look endured till the show's 1989 demise.

Colonel Sanders
DRESSED FOR SUCCESS

In 1952, at age 62, Col. Harland Sanders began franchising his fried chicken recipe to existing restaurant owners and earning a nickel on every bird sold. In a decade the Colonel built a multimillion-dollar empire—one so tied to his own image that the IRS allowed him to deduct the cost of his white suits as a business expense.

SHOCK TR

Some performers ranged from wild and rebellious to "what were they thinking?" But while leaving us shaking our heads, they seared their indelible images on our memories

Phyllis Diller
ONE FOR THE AGES

She was a 37-year-old mother of five before ever setting foot onstage. "I was the woman-next-door," Diller, now 84, once recalled. "But people don't want to pay to see the woman-next-door." As her career evolved, so did her appearance. The hair got bushier, the costumes more out-landish. But with several plastic surgeries, her face remained strangely constant.

Cyndi Lauper
SO UNUSUAL

One of MTV's first stars, Lauper was as big on visuals as on sound. Her voice was pitch-perfect ban-shee, but her '80s wardrobe seemed culled from a thrift-shop explosion. She continues to employ a rainbow of hair dye ("I get bored") but has tamed her flamboyant ways. "Up close," she said recently of the old look, "it kind of freaked me out."

EATMENT

Janis Joplin
THE SHOWGIRL

Having fled the oppressive, bouffant South of the '60s, Joplin flourished in San Francisco. Willing to show more than just a little piece of her heart, the hard-living blues rock queen favored sheer fabrics, yards of beads and boas with more feathers than a country bed.

David Bowie
THE ALIEN

From *Space Oddity* to *Ziggy Stardust,* Bowie adorned his '70s "just visiting" persona with unearthly glamour and androgyny. Defending his early frocks, he said, "They were men's dresses. They didn't have big boobs or anything."

Marlon Brando
WITHOUT A CAUSE

"What are you rebelling against?" asks a woman in 1954's *The Wild One.* Brando's biker replies, "What've you got?" Delivered in jeans and a leather jacket, his attitude made both synonymous with rebellion. Now, of course, they are staples at the Gap.

Jimi Hendrix
Do Not Try This at Home

If you are a guitar god, you can give your tailor instructions like these, which Hendrix once jotted for his: "Use your wise judgment and imagination. Make as many shirts as you can: different colors, patterns, even crocheting [and] shirts with odd sleeves . . ." The rest of you: J. Crew.

Prince
Wearing Blender

Nodding to Rick James, Liberace and Louis XIV, Prince (in the early '80s) made paisley, fedoras and heels his own. Oddly, designer Betsey Johnson credited Prince's mix with helping women to "want to look like women again."

Grace Jones
Self-Made Woman

This was a getup from 1984's *Conan the Destroyer,* but it wasn't far from the singer-actress's real-life harness. "You create yourself," she said. "You're not born this way. I didn't look strange when I was young."

Liberace
MUSIC'S STRAIGHT MAN

Look, if you plunk down in front of a mirrored piano in a 137-pound blue mink and more rings than a redwood, people will snicker. But for Wladziu Valentino Liberace (in 1984), showmanship was no joke. As his sister Angelina saw it, "He doesn't much care for the real world, you know?"

Dennis Rodman
THE COLOR GUARD

In the Michael Jordan era, a mere gifted athlete needed an extra to distinguish himself. For the Worm, it was neon hair and the occasional gown. "If he's got the intestinal fortitude to put on a wedding dress, more power to him," said a fellow NBA'er. "Can you fault the guy for wanting to make a dollar?"

Elton John
SIGHT FOR FOUR EYES

To focus on his celebrated eyeglasses is, well, nearsighted. Sir Elton (in 1974) is a package from plumed tête to platformed toe. Naturally, it's mostly made for him. But he's also a tireless shopper: "I can find a store in the desert."

Boy George
PRETTY BABY

He wrapped a man's white soul voice in braids and geisha makeup, and somehow pulled it off. The proof was in the rise of his '80s band, Culture Club. Years after its demise, he shared old photos with pals and joked, "You let me go out like that?"

Gwen Stefani
COLORFAST

The Shiva–meets–Cookie Monster look was brief for the No Doubt singer. Usually, she pairs gym togs with full-glam makeup. Dresses, she says, make her look "like a piece of candy."

Björk
FASHION LEDA

Her mythmaking 2001 Oscar outfit caused some to crack that she'd been dressed by the near-blind woman she played in *Dancer in the Dark*. The Icelandic star didn't see the fuss: "It's just a dress!"

Lil' Kim
MADE YOU LOOK

She had been in hip-hop since 1996, but only at the 1999 MTV video awards (below) did Kim become a household name. "Sex sells," she noted after the notorious broadcast. "This is my image. I don't walk the streets like that."

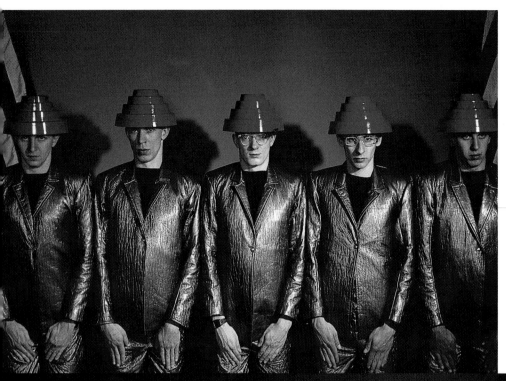

Devo
REVENGE OF THE NERDS

Looking as manufactured as their synthesized music, these Akron, Ohio, art students became late-'70s new-wave darlings. Onstage they favored plastic lab coats. "I used to lose three or four pounds a night," recalled bassist Gerald Casale.

Kiss
…AND MAKE UP

Besides their 1976 anthem "Rock and Roll All Nite," most people can't name a Kiss tune. The band's strength was its lacquered glam-metal characters, easily reproduced as dolls or on thermoses. Let other bands flaunt their integrity. "Face it," said Gene Simmons (tongue out), "who wants an R.E.M. lunchbox, no matter how much you like the music?"

The Sex Pistols
GOD SAVE ... MY JEANS?

In the 25 years since punk tore through Britain, cultural critics have variously deconstructed the symbolism of the Sex Pistols' predilection for safety pins. But Sid Vicious (left, with Johnny Rotten) claimed they were simply a way to salvage a pair of pants that had been shredded. Explaining away their enthusiasm for drawing their own blood in concert was a bit tougher.

Nirvana
FASHION ANTIHEROES

Flannel shirts are just good sense in chilly Seattle. When bands from the area went national, they brought along their casual aesthetic, dubbed grunge, as was their music. Nirvana's threadbare rags and unwashed hair suggested they didn't care about fame. But, charged a Seattle music journalist, "Kurt Cobain [center, in 1993 with Kris Novoselic and Dave Grohl] was just too lazy to shampoo." Soon after, grunge turned up in *Vogue*.

Run DMC
THE PIONEERS

Warm-up gear worn with ropy gold chains is now to rap attire what the gray flannel suit and suspenders once were to Wall Street. Run DMC were largely responsible for developing their musical genre as well as its dress code. In 2000, 14 years after their hit "My Adidas" came out, a pair of sneakers worn by DMC, a.k.a. Darryl McDaniels (left, with Run [Joseph Simmons] and Jam Master Jay [Jason Mizell]), was enshrined in the Rock and Roll Hall of Fame.

Hair

Bold as Sinéad's coif
or big as Dolly's—
a singular sensation
is one way to turn
your name into a
showbiz brand

Sinéad O'Connor
THE MINIMALIST

Record execs wanted to package that big voice with equally soaring hair. O'Connor thought otherwise, and in 1987 shaved it all off, saying, "I didn't want to sell myself on my physicality."

Dolly Parton
SIZE MATTERS

Thank God she's a country girl. How else to explain all this excess but with her down-home quip: "It takes a lot of money to look this cheap." Parton's look (and her 300 wigs) made her the perfect choice to play the hairdresser in *Steel Magnolias* (1989), who affirms, "There is no such thing as natural beauty."

Suzanne Somers
OFF KILTER

To play Chrissy, *Three's Company*'s dippiest roommate, Somers topped her blank-as-a-page stare with a seriously dumb do. The asymmetrical ponytail sprung from her head like an alien's antenna, searching, unsuccessfully, for intelligent signs of life below.

Shaun Cassidy
WINGING IT

Following in the wake of his half brother David, Cassidy became a late-'70s teen dream with a TV show (*The Hardy Boys*) and lite hits like "Da Do Run Run." Most important, he stayed faithful to David's feathery, blown coif.

Jennifer Aniston
SHAGADELIC

Fans had barely learned Aniston's name when they began bringing her photo to hair salons, demanding her cute, modern shag. But after seven seasons of longer and shorter versions of the style, Aniston lopped it into a bob. "I did it mainly to relieve me of the bondage of self," she told *Vanity Fair*. But the new cut, she admitted, is "just not me."

Crystal Gayle
THE LONG HAUL

"What I hate most is Velcro," she says. "I've lost a lot of hair to Velcro." Not so as we'd notice. Her sister Loretta Lynn may have the more celebrated singing career—weren't they *both* coal miner's daughters?—but Gayle went to far greater lengths to be remembered for her singular appearance.

Some like it girly, others curly. Showbiz history is a chronicle of do's—and don'ts

Tom Hanks
HIS FEMININE SIDE

The '70s had just ended, but Hanks kept his 'fro to play Kip Wilson and Buffy, a woman he becomes in order to get a cheap room in a female residence on *Bosom Buddies*. Hanks said he took roles like this—and, later, the coach in *A League of Their Own*—to spread the word that he'll "do anything. Get fat. Cut [my] hair in an unattractive manner. I don't have to be the king of every scene."

Robert Reed
HAIR-CURLING MYSTERY

In the pilot for *The Brady Bunch*, Reed has straight hair. Later, this. Perm, perchance? "The jury's out," said Barry Williams, who played the oldest Brady son. "We went to Hawaii, and he said it was the humidity."

James Brown
HARDEST-WORKING HAIR

"Hair and teeth—if a man got those two things, he got it all," said Brown at 60. For decades, he has begun every show with a perfect pompadour. But after spinning and *Yow!*ing, he leaves his killer smile to do all the work, because his hair is done for the night.

Kid 'N Play
HERE COME OLD FLATTOP

Though they had four albums and made three films together, the jocular rappers Kid 'N Play may be best known for Kid's gravity-defying hair—at one point it topped four feet. For three years the style begged stupid questions, and Kid (left) fielded them with humor: "No, I was never in physical pain—unless the doorway was low." Then, in 1992, he cut it, declaring, "Enough."

It's become a world where dreads and beads can rule, and Beatty cruised and conquered with a blow-dryer

Bob Marley
LOCK JOCK

His lushly matted dreadlocks took the Jamaican singer years to cultivate. But the slow growth had long-lasting repercussions. Novelist Alice Walker (*The Color Purple*) remembered seeing Marley in photos. "I couldn't imagine those black ropes were hair," she wrote. "Natural hair to which nothing is added, not even a brushing." Walker eventually adopted the look herself. "Bob Marley is the person who taught me to trust the universe enough to respect my hair."

Venus Williams
SMASHING BEAUTY

Before they hear the thwack of racket clobbering ball, Williams' competitors might catch the clicking sound of swinging beads. They should come with a warning: Don't let them distract you from the strokes of the 6'2" elder Williams sister. At the U.S. Open (which she won in 2000) her beads were red, white and blue. At Wimbledon she wore that tournament's colors: purple, white and green. But Williams has warned reporters, "I don't want to talk about my hair."

The Mod Squad
Black, White and Blonde

Three juvenile delinquents enlisted by the L.A. Police Department—well, of course they're going to have great hair. Pete (Michael Cole) bore a hippie helmet. Linc (Clarence Williams III) went for a monster Afro. And Julie (Peggy Lipton) sported the most sublime straight, limp locks on '60s TV.

Warren Beatty
Stylist Behind the Stylist

In 1975 Beatty needed hair that looked like 1968 (the year *Shampoo* was set) and that held up under a motorcycle helmet. His shag was created by Kathryn Blondell, credited lately with Tom Hanks's un-do in *Castaway*.

Whoopi Goldberg
Supernatural

"Low maintenance" is how Goldberg (née Caryn Johnson) justified allowing her hair to develop into a her now-familiar "natural. But for so long, my particular package was alien to everybody. Today when I see dreads, braids, plum lipstick and women wearing flats and sneakers, I know part of that is because of me."

Bo Derek
Tough Rows to Hoe

Blake Edwards cast Derek in 1979's *10,* but it was her husband, John, who suggested the cornrows—as if anyone would be looking at her hair. Okay, white women did, flocking to African-American braiding parlors to get a look long-popular with blacks. But not everyone could be Bo. Reported one stylist: "There are a lot of 5's around here trying to look like 10's."

Linda Evangelista
CUTTING HER LOSSES

In 1988 she had a respectable modeling career, but not stardom. Then a photographer proposed losing the long hair. Evangelista's mom advised her not to, arguing, "Everybody has long hair." Hmm, Linda agreed, everybody did. So she went for it and soon could afford to quip, "I don't get out of bed for less than $10,000 a day."

Mia Farrow
SHORT CUT TO FAME

Born to director John Farrow and *Tarzan* star Maureen O'Sullivan, and engaged to Frank Sinatra at 20, the actress had yet to break out on her own, or from behind a wall of long hair. Then, before a 1965 episode of *Peyton Place,* she traded her adolescent tresses for a chic pixie cap. The style gave Mia her own buzz and, later refined by Vidal Sassoon, earned new glory in *Rosemary's Baby*.

Dorothy Hamill
THE SHORT PROGRAM

It sounded like a skating move: the wedge. If every suburban girl cutting figure eights in the rink at the mall couldn't have a medal, they could at least have the most popular haircut of 1976. Four years later the retired Olympic gold medalist remained a very photographed (and modest) woman. "I don't know what the camera sees in me," Hamill said then. "I don't look like Bo Derek or Farrah Fawcett. I might like to, but beggars can't be choosy."

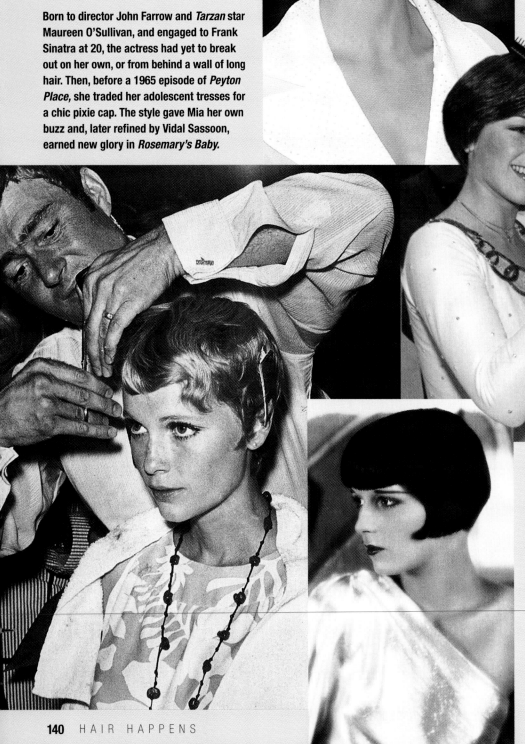

Louise Brooks
FLAPPER FLAP

"She was way too wild," said an admirer, "in a business that was way too tame." Beneath the actress's neat bobbed cap of hair was a no-frills head for moviemaking and an ahead-of-her-time sexual freedom. In the late '20s, when silent films gave way to more expensive talkies, studios asked several players to take a pay cut. Brooks refused, instead moving her career to Europe. She returned but, still regarded as a threat by Hollywood, settled for modest success writing.

Keri Russell
A LONG STORY

"She's so gorgeous, we thought, 'Who cares how long her hair is?'" recalled *Felicity* producer J.J. Abrams. A lot of people, it turned out. A hit when it launched in 1998, the show fell in the ratings during its sophomore season when Russell, who plays the title character, lopped off her cascading curls. The actress said she preferred her hair that way, not realizing her fans would not. Angry e-mails and letters flooded *Felicity*'s production offices. "I don't [identify with] that person," wrote one distressed woman. "It ruins the illusion." Before the start of the third season, WB network entertainment president Susanne Daniels reassured viewers, "It's growing." With Russell's hair down to her shoulders, ratings went back up. Said Daniels: "Nobody is cutting their hair again on this network."

Shirley Temple
LORD OF THE RINGLETS

Temple's mother, Gertrude, the woman who stood next to film directors instructing her child to "sparkle," was also responsible for rolling the 56 sausage curls that framed the young star's cherubic face. Those ringlets, and that sparkle, made Shirley the top box office attraction throughout the 1930s. Across the country a lot of other little girls sat still while their own mothers fought with the curlers, all trying to get that Temple look. Any easier way? Purchase her then-popular doll.

To wannabes who will go to any length to please, careers ride on the final cut

INDEX

PICTURE CREDITS

Front Cover (Julia Roberts) Brigitte Lacombe • (Princess Diana) Jim Spellman/Ipol • (Madonna) Gerardo Somoza/CorbisOutline • (Elvis Presley) Photoplay Archives/Corbis • (Jacqueline Kennedy Onassis) Steve Shaw/Photo Researchers • (Oprah Winfrey) Walter McBride/Retna

50 Greatest Style Setters 4-5 (from left) Bettmann/Corbis; Bob Willoughby/MPTV; Michael Ochs Archives.com; Photofest; Peter Kramer/Star Max; Pier Luigi/Rex • 6-7 (clockwise from left) MPTV; George Zeno Collection; Archive Photos (2); Robert Wolders/Sygma/Corbis • 8-9 (clockwise from left) Mark Shaw/Photo Researchers; Bettmann/Corbis; Express Newspapers/Archive Photos; Brian Quigley/CorbisOutline; Bettmann/Corbis • 10-11 (clockwise from bottom right) Robin Nunn/Nunn Syndication; David Hartley/RDR/Rex; Ken Goff/Timepix; Tim Graham/Sygma/Corbis; Jayne Fincher/Photographers Int'l/CorbisOutline • 12-13 (clockwise from top right) Bill Davila/Retna; Ernie Stewart/Retna; Adrian Groom/In-Focus/Newsmakers; Bill Davila/Retna; Gary Hershorn/Reuters • 14-15 (clockwise from top right) Bettmann/Corbis; Sasha/Archive Photos; Hulton-Deutsch Collection/Corbis; H. Roger Viollet/Liaison • 16 Neal Peters Collection • 17 (from top) Everett Collection; Bettmann/Corbis; Photofest; Bettmann/Corbis • 18-19 (from left) David Fisher/LFI; Paul Smith/Featureflash/Retna (2); Dave Hogan/RDR/Rex • 20 (clockwise from top left) Eric Pendzich/RDR/Rex; David Allocca/DMI/Timepix; Mitchell Gerber/Corbis; Anthony Dixon/LFI; Kevin Winter/Celebrity Photo; Paul Smith/Featureflash/Retna; Scott Downie/Celebrity Photo • 21 Photofest • 22 MPTV • 23 (from top) MPTV; Sanford Roth/MPTV; Bettmann/Corbis • 24 Shooting Star • 25 (from top) MPTV; Popperfoto/Archive Photos; AFP/Corbis • 26-27 (from left) Joseph Cultice/CorbisOutline; Kwaku Alston/CorbisOutline; Reuters/Steve Marcus/Archive Photos; Fitzroy Barrett/Globe Photos • 28 Glen Embree/MPTV • 29 (from top) Bettmann/Corbis; E.R. Richee/MPTV • 30-31 (clockwise from right) David Allocca/DMI/Timepix; Bill Davila/Retna; Peter Kramer/Star Max; AFP/Corbis; Kevin Horan/CorbisOutline • 32 Shooting Star • 33 (from top) Chierichette Collection/Shooting Star; Alfred Eisenstaedt/Timepix; Sunset BD/Sygma/Corbis • 34 (from top) David Sutton/MPTV; JSP/Shooting Star; Richard Miller/MPTV • 35 Richard Miller/MPTV • 36 Lester Cohen/Shooting Star • 37 Everett Collection • 38 Cliff Watts/Icon • 39 (from top) AFP/Corbis; Wyatt Counts/CorbisOutline; Reuters NewMedia/Corbis • 40 Kobal Collection • 41 Neal Preston/Corbis • 42-43 (clockwise from top right) Michael Ochs Archives.com (2); Eve Arnold/Magnum Photos; Michael Ochs Archives.com; Photofest • 44 John Launois/Black Star • 45 CBS Photo Archive/Archive Photos; Everett Collection; Michael Ochs Archives.com • 46 Ken Whitmore/MPTV; (inset) Gary Lewis/Camera Press/Retna • 47 Ken Regan/Camera 5; (inset) MPTV • 48 Denis Reggie • 49 (from top) John Barrett/Globe Photos; Alex Oliveira/RDR/Rex; Mike Segar/Newsmakers • 50 Steve Finn/Globe Photos • 51 Sporting News/Archive Photos; (inset) Reuters/Sue Ogrocki/Archive Photos • 52 Stephanie Cardinale/Sygma/Corbis • 53 Gjon Mili/Timepix 54-55 (clockwise from top right) Michael Ochs Archives.com; Kevin Mazur/Wire Image; Richard Young/Rex; Adam Scull/Globe Photos; Neal Preston/CorbisOutline • 56 Ken Probst/CorbisOutline • 57 Women's Wear Daily • 58 Sid Avery/MPTV • 59 (from top) Archive Photos; CBS Photo Archive/Archive Photos; Archive Photos • 60 Richard Wright/CorbisOutline • 61 Ron Davis/Shooting Star • 62 Bert Six/MPTV • 63 Bettmann/Corbis • 64-65 (clockwise from right) Art Streiber/Icon; Reuters NewMedia/Corbis; Lisa Means; Mark Liddell/Icon • 66 Mick Hutson/Redferns/Retna • 67 (from top) Reuters/Gary Hershorn/Archive Photos; Bill Davila/Retna; Phil Knott/Camera Press/Retna; Rafael Fuchs/CorbisOutline • 68 Andrew Eccles/CorbisOutline • 69 James Globus/CorbisOutline • 70 Brigitte Lacombe • 71 (from top) Lisa Rose/JPI; Steve Granitz/Retna; Craig Blankenhorn/MPTV • 72-73 Charles Bush/Everett Collection • 74-75 (clockwise from left) E.J. Camp/CorbisOutline; Harry Langdon/Shooting Star (2); Neal Preston/Corbis; Harry Langdon/Shooting Star (2); CBS Photo Archive; Steve Granitz/Retna; Reuters/Rose Prouser/Archive Photos • 76 Neal Preston/Corbis • 77 Burt Glinn/Magnum Photos • 78-79 (from left) AFP/Corbis; Dave Hogan/All Action/Retna; Celebrity Photo; Stephen Trupp/Star Max; Robert Sebree • 80 Michael Ochs Archives.com • 81 Albert Sanchez/CorbisOutline • 82-83 (top left) Mattel; (left to right) Mattel; Sygma/Corbis; Mattel; Sygma/Corbis; Globe Photos; Ron Avery/MPTV

Top 10's 84-85 (clockwise from top right) Gerardo Somoza/CorbisOutline; Ron Davis/Shooting Star; Jonathan Alcorn/Zuma Press; Donato Sardella/Women's Wear Daily; Steve Granitz/Retna; Lisa Rose/JPI; Paul Smith/Featureflash/Retna; Kathy Hutchins/Hutchins Photo; Los Angeles Daily News/Saga/Archive Photos; Walter Weissman/Globe Photos; Sam Jones/CorbisOutline; Reuters/Jack Daboghian/Archive Photos • 86-87 (clockwise from top left) Gerardo Somoza/CorbisOutline; Steffen Thalemann/CorbisOutline; Andrea Renault/Globe Photos; Reuters/Timepix; Andrea Renault/Globe Photos (2); Liza Rose/Globe Photos; courtesy Tommy Hilfiger; Jim Smeal/Galella/Gamma; Fitzroy Barrett/Globe Photos; Jeff Kravitz/Film Magic; Lisa Rose/Globe Photos; 88-89 (clockwise from top right) Joe Gaffney/Retna; Neal Peters Collection; Lynn Goldsmith/Corbis; Sonia Moskowitz/Globe Photos; Photofest; Globe Photos • 90-91 (clockwise from left) Neal Peters Collection; Photofest; Walter Weissman/Globe Photos; courtesy Nolan Miller; Photofest; Dirck Halstead/Timepix • 92-93 (clockwise from left) King Collection/Retna; Walter Iooss Jr./Sports Illustrated; Charlotte MacPherson/Camera Press/Retna; Robert Fairer/Retna; SMP/Globe Photos • 94-95 (from left) Norman Parkinson Ltd./Fiona Cowan/Corbis; BVD/Corbis; Michael Childers/Sygma/Corbis; Maria Valentino/MCV (2)

Girl Power 96-97 (clockwise from top left) Photofest; Bettmann/Corbis; F. Meylan/Sygma/Corbis; Richard Cartwright/WB • 98-99 (top right) Sony Classic Pictures; Photofest (4) • 100-101 (clockwise from bottom right) Photofest; Kobal Collection (3); Bettmann/Corbis; Foto Fantasies • 102 (from top) Lynn Goldsmith/Corbis; Neal Peters Collection; Kobal Collection • 103 (from top) Will Hart/Sports Illustrated; Photofest

A Brief History of Blonde 104-105 (from left) Michael Ochs Archives.com; ABC/Photofest; MPTV • 106-107 (clockwise from top right) Tom Caffery/Globe Photos; JSP/Shooting Star; Deborah Feingold/CorbisOutline; Michael Ochs Archives.com • 108-109 (clockwise from top left) Steve Granitz/Retna; George Zeno Collection; Henry Gross/FPG; Kate Garner/Visages; Photofest; George Lange/CorbisOutline • 110-111 (clockwise from top right) Glenn Watson/MPTV; Nick Baratta; Tama Herrick/Zuma/Timepix; Bill Davila/Retna; Photofest • 112 (from top) E.J. Camp/CorbisOutline; Gwendolyn Cates • 113 MPTV (3) • 114 (from top) Stephen Wayda/CorbisOutline; FPG • 115 (from top) Waring Abbott/Michael Ochs Archives.com; Tammie Arroyo/Camera Press/Retna; Bernard Kuhmstedt/CorbisOutline

Red Zone 116-117 (from left) Deborah Feingold/CorbisOutline; Don Ornitz/Globe Photos; Sid Avery/MPTV • 118-119 (from left) Gabi Rona/MPTV; Peter Nash/CorbisOutline; Photofest; Steve Finn/Globe Photos; Shooting Star • 120-121 (clockwise from top right) NBC/Globe Photos; MPTV; Shooting Star; Photofest; Robert Eric/Sygma/Corbis; George Holz/CorbisOutline

Men in White 122-123 (from left) Guy Aroch/CorbisOutline; Michael O'Neill/CorbisOutline; Movie Still Archives • 124-125 (clockwise from top right) Bettmann/Corbis; Photofest (2); Sid Avery/MPTV; Wallace Seawell/MPTV; Andy Freeberg/Retna; Bettmann/Corbis

Shock Treatment 126 Photofest • 127 Tony Costa/CorbisOutline • 128 (from left) Neal Preston/Corbis; MPTV; Photofest • 129 (from top) Ed Caraeff; Ross Marino/Sygma/Corbis; Michael Childers/Sygma/Corbis • 130-131 (clockwise from top right) Mirek Towski/DMI/Timepix; Reuters NewMedia/Corbis; Kevin Mazur/LFI; Michael O'Neill/CorbisOutline; John Seakwood/CorbisOutline; Bregman/MPTV; T. O'Neill/Sygma/Corbis • 132-133 (clockwise from top right) Lynn Goldsmith/Corbis; Chris Cuffaro/CorbisOutline; Ilpo Musto/LFI; Claude Van Heye/LFI; Photofest

Hair Happens 134 Deborah Feingold/CorbisOutline • 135 Barbara Walz/CorbisOutline • 136-137 (clockwise from top right) Photofest; MPTV; Janette Beckman/CorbisOutline; Globe Photos; Photofest; Lynn Goldsmith/Corbis; MPTV; Ralph Dominguez/Globe Photos • 138-139 (clockwise from top right) Photofest; Ellen Graham/Sygma/Corbis; Bruce McBroom/MPTV; Nancy Rica Schiff/SAGA/Archive Photos; Brian Smith/CorbisOutline; David Corio/Michael Ochs Archives.com • 140 (from top) Maria Valentino/MCV; Bettmann/Corbis; MPTV (2) • 141 (from top) Jeff Slocomb/CorbisOutline; Challenge Roddie/CorbisOutline; Kean/Doolittle/MPTV